*Philadelphia
and the China Trade,
1682–1846*

Bronze bas-relief on pedestal of
Stephen Girard statue formerly at City
Hall Plaza, Philadelphia. Girard is
shown observing his packet ship *Rousseau*, which was active in the China
trade.

Philadelphia
and the China Trade
1682–1846

Commercial, Cultural,
and Attitudinal Effects

Jonathan Goldstein

The Pennsylvania State University Press

University Park and London

This volume was published with the
cooperation and support of the Pennsylvania
Historical and Museum Commission in its
continuing attempt to preserve the history
of the people of the Commonwealth.

Library of Congress Cataloging in Publication Data

Goldstein, Jonathan.
  Philadelphia and the China trade, 1682–1846.

  Originally presented as the author's thesis, University of Pennsylvania.
  Bibliography: p. 103
  Includes index.   1.   Philadelphia—Commerce—China—History.
2.   China—Commerce—Philadelphia—History.   I.   Title.
HF3163.P5G64 1977   382′.09748′11051   77-1638
ISBN 0-271-00512-2

Designed by Glenn Ruby

Printed in the United States of America

Contents

Foreword

It is a pleasure to introduce Jonathan Goldstein's first book to the world of scholarship. *Philadelphia and the China Trade, 1682–1846* is a happy combination of assiduous archival research and a delightful cultural sensitivity. The author began his research by immersing himself in the then recently opened Stephen Girard Papers. He found them immensely rich on China-trade matters and, somewhat to his surprise, he found that they did not seem to forecast the racism which was later to poison American-Chinese relations and lead to the exclusion of Chinese immigrants in 1882 and after. Girard, for example, had high respect and esteem for the co-hong traders with whom he dealt at Canton.

From the Girard Papers treasury, the author broadened his research to other East Coast archives, which he combed for every shred of information he could obtain about Philadelphia's China trade, as well as contemporary published sources and secondary works. He analyzed every voyage from Philadelphia to China by whatever route during the period of his study. In addition he took into account cultural evidence which he discovered in museums and private collections.

His general conclusion that Philadelphians in particular and East Coast Americans in general were not only enthusiastically interested in the China trade but had warm feelings for the Chinese and their culture is supported by an immense amount of research and analysis.

Regardless of broader issues concerning American attitudes toward China and the Chinese, the present study provides a wealth of detail on early interactions between America and China. It shows how certain American fortunes waxed and waned on the trade as its patterns changed. Of special interest in this regard is a substantial discussion of the role of Philadelphia merchants in the opium trade, giving the amounts involved, the names of those who engaged in it and those who did not, and the arguments both sides used to defend or condemn participation in it. The analysis provides an intimate view not only of the opium question itself but of its ramifications in terms of the tensions it caused with the Chinese government, while at the same time it is kept in the perspective of the much larger, in terms of Philadelphia at least, trade in other commodities.

Finally, the author's judicious selection of illustrations may be noted. Taken from museum pieces or contemporary works, they have the flavor of the period. Where else can one find a ginseng root, a Chinese cotton plant, and a Turkish opium plant drawn in fine line detail? Or a "Chinese cottage" in Mt. Holly, New Jersey?

There are many treasures in Dr. Goldstein's book, and it is a pleasure to commend it to the reading public.

Hilary Conroy

University of Pennsylvania

Chinese bamboo

Preface

In the eighteenth and first half of the nineteenth centuries, in the absence of diplomatic relations or any other official contacts between Americans and Chinese, Philadelphia merchants established extensive relationships with their Chinese counterparts. This book, based primarily on documentary sources, traces the evolution of those ties from 1682, when Philadelphia port was established, until 1846, when the first Sino-American treaty went into effect and fundamentally restructured the relationships that had been evolving in an informal manner during the preceding 164 years.

The book examines the comparatively neglected question of how, in an era before modern means of transportation and communication, a brisk sea trade developed between Philadelphia's aspiring entrepreneurs and a nation on the other side of the globe. The book is also intended to throw light on the relationship between East and West at large. How did an American merchant community react to a civilization which was in many respects as culturally different from it as it was geographically remote? How were the arts and technology of China appraised and utilized in an early American city? To what extent did "racist" views permeate this intercultural interaction, and with what effect, if any, on subsequent Chinese-American relations?

Prepared originally as a dissertation at the University of Pennsylvania, this study was in large measure inspired by two professors who guided me toward the field of American relations with East Asia long before the subject assumed its current popularity. Allyn Rickett's firsthand commentary on the course of modern Chinese history induced me to choose East Asia as a region of concentration. My most difficult task in the academic process—the committing of ideas into written argument—has been eased through Hilary Conroy's kindly and patient supervision of both this study and its predecessor, my Senior Honors Thesis on Stephen Girard's China trade. This book has also benefited from the bibliographical assistance and warm encouragement of Murphey Smith of the American Philosophical Society, from the textual criticism of Jacques Downs of Saint Francis College, and from the editorial assistance and typing of Doris Sklaroff.

In addition to Messrs. Smith and Downs, many scholars and librarians have assisted in ferreting out the arcane materials needed for this study. For their research help, I wish to thank: Lee Houchins, Research Associate, Smithsonian Institution; Peter Parker, Historical Society of Pennsylvania; Lillian Tonkin, Library Company of Philadelphia; Robert Schwarz and Phyllis Abrams, Girard College; Francis Lothrop, Peabody Museum of Salem; and the entire University of Pennsylvania library staff.

Grants-in-aid from the Bureau of Archives and History of the Pennsylvania Historical and Museum Commission and from the American Philosophical Society have also facilitated the completion of this study.

Lastly, I owe an inestimable debt of gratitude to those members of my family who, by their inspiration, their encouragement, and most of all their example, made many hot summers in Philadelphia that much more bearable, and who made this book, and my entire career and development, possible. I therefore dedicate this study to my mother, Miriam Sargon, and to the cherished memories of my father, David Goldstein, and my grandmother, Lena Saltz Bludman.

List of Illustrations

Common blue-and-white porcelain bowl. Jon Peter Hulleberg.

Mounted silk samples from the Canton merchant Eshing. The Peabody Museum of Salem.

Armorial porcelain mug. Illustration Phil. Cooke Collection.

Monogrammed porcelain bowl. Estate of Stephen Girard, dec'd, Philadelphia, Pennsylvania.

Custom-made punch bowl. The Pennsylvania Hospital.

The Ship *Montesquieu,* by the Painter of "The Wreck of the President Adams." Estate of Stephen Girard, dec'd, Philadelphia, Pennsylvania.

The Crew of the *Alliance* in Canton.

Lacquered tea chest. Estate of Stephen Girard, dec'd, Philadelphia, Pennsylvania.

Turkish opium plant. Pier Mattioli, *Commentarii in VI Libros de Medica Materia,* II (Venice: Apud Felicem Vargrisium, 1583).

Nathan Dunn's "Chinese Cottage," Mount Holly, New Jersey, 1832. Designed by John Notman. Drawing from A. J. Downing, *A Treatise on the Theory and Practice of Landscape Gardening* (New York and London: Wiley and Putnam, 1841). Library Company of Philadelphia.

China, by Robert Waln, Jr. Library Company of Philadelphia.

Chinese "varnish tree." Jean Du Halde, *A Description of China,* I (London: T. Gardner, 1738).

Chinese cotton tree. Jean Du Halde, *A Description of China,* I (London: T. Gardner, 1738).

Chinese tea shrub

1 Commercial and Social Issues of the China Trade, and the Philadelphia Experience

China has long been one of the richest, that is, one of the most fertile, best cultivated, most industrious, most populous countries in the world.

—Adam Smith[1]

In 1836, the 300 block of Walnut Street, Philadelphia, exuded the prosperity which had favored this seaport city in the 154 years since its founding. Although the block began unostentatiously enough, at the corner of Fourth Street, with a colonial home adorned only with a simple wooden pediment above the front door, one's eyes were inextricably drawn down the row of formidably chimneyed merchants' residences to the Episcopal bishop's manse, with enscrolled attic windows, doric-pillared portal, and inset half-moon glass. Just beyond the bishop's house, across Third Street, stood the Greek-revival facade of the Philadelphia Exchange. In this newly completed temple, businessmen met to barter or sell the cargoes and merchandise which had become the source of the new urban wealth.

While exteriors of these buildings reflected the increasing afflu-
ence of the harbor town, if one were to step inside some of them, an
additional dimension of prosperity would emerge. On entering the
foyer of the John Latimer residence, for example, at 359 Walnut,
one might have been startled, at first, when confronted by a large oil
painting depicting a terrible fire in various stages of ravaging a large
port city. Was this a forewarning of the nemesis awaiting rich Philadelphians? Although an American flag could be discerned flying
above one of the houses in the painting, further observation revealed that the port being depicted was not Penn's town. Boatmen
shown fleeing the destruction were not Caucasians, but Chinese in
junks. This was not a Quaker's apocalyptic vision, but rather a Chinese port painter's renditions of the harbor of Canton, China, during a recent conflagration.

If the onlooker was perplexed by the existence of Chinese sea-
scapes in an early American home, his amazement could only have
been heightened by the display in the Latimer library: Chinese porcelain teacups, saucers, milk and teapots, sugar dish and stand, and
tea canister—each item with a colorful "Canton" or "Nanking"
border. The pantry shelves bore a still larger assortment of willow-
ware dinner sets, each piece showing an Oriental willow tree spring-
ing from a tiny river island. A fine corner cupboard in the dining
room was reserved for ceramic pieces decorated with the coats of
arms and monograms of various Latimer family members. This
room also exhibited large medallion ware vases and two nests of
intricately carved Chinese rosewood tables. In the dimly lit upper
hallway, atop a washstand, one could perceive the glistening of Chinese lacquered toilet articles, in purple and gold.[2]

Walnut Street, then, boasted more than opulence: there was an
Oriental flavor to that opulence. While one scholar has calculated
that an early nineteenth-century Boston or Salem dwelling might
have had one-tenth to one-fifth of its effects from China, some
Philadelphia residences fell not far short of that estimate.[3] The Chinese influence in the Philadelphia region, furthermore, was not
confined to the posh houses of the inner city. The majority of Chinese articles shipped to early Pennsylvania were found in poorer
homes. The commoner grades of porcelain, along with misfires,
were transported to Philadelphia as ballast, and then sold. The average family could fill its ceramic vessels with a wide variety of Chinese
teas, and could also occasionally partake of exotic crystallized ginger
candy or Chinese cinnamon, a substitute for the more expensive
spice from Ceylon.[4]

In an era before textile manufacturing had developed in the

United States, Nanking cotton cloth, a brownish yellow weave of firm texture and great durability, served, along with native American homespun, as the workaday fabric of early America. "Nankeen," as it was called, was used particularly in making trousers. For good wear, common Pennsylvanians could indulge in an occasional Chinese-made jacket, vest, embroidered shawl, umbrella, paper fan, or pair of shoes.

In short, Philadelphians of all social classes availed themselves of the talents of the extraordinary merchant and craftsman community of Canton, China, and its environs. This community—painters working in oil, watercolor, enamel, and lacquer; weavers, embroiderers, tailors, shoe and umbrella makers; silversmiths and other metal workers; carvers, gilders, and cabinet makers—produced, in the opinion of one expert, "more goods of consistently high quality and good taste, in greater variety over a longer period of time, than any other artisan community the world has ever known."[5] The influence of this commerce went well beyond the mere presence of Oriental articles in Quaker City dwellings. In the case of many businessmen of Philadelphia, and other early American cities, the trade in Chinese commodities was the very basis of wealth, the means whereby a Walnut Street or some other town house, or country estate, or cotton mill, or railroad, could be acquired.

This study will examine the commercial and also the social aspects of Philadelphia's China trade. Since these topics are inextricably tied together, it is impossible to isolate them into separate sections. Both themes will be regularly referred to, in a consideration of how Philadelphia's businessmen came to develop and prosper from Oriental trade, and also how they perceived their contact with a different culture.

The commercial aspect of Philadelphia's China trade has been a comparatively neglected topic in historical writing, and this study can therefore fill a lacuna in early American business history. The social history of the early contact has been examined by scholars, but there are conflicting views on what actually occurred. This study may furnish additional data and also serve as a test of these conflicting views.

The question of why American historians have traditionally ignored non-Western civilizations, even those which, like China, have influenced the development of our own culture, is an intriguing one, but beyond the purview of this study.[6] The limited observation can be made that the China trade from Philadelphia, the nation's capital, largest port, most populous city, and intellectual center during much of early American history, is a topic heretofore largely unexamined in the literature of American business history.[7] Even the two maritime histories of Philadelphia give the trade scant analysis,[8] and Ann White's unpublished research paper on Philadelphia's China trade did not discuss Philadelphia merchants' opening and development of the American opium trade to China.[9]

This extant body of literature leaves several questions unanswered:

1. What was the importance of the trade in tea, and other Chinese commodities, to pre-Revolutionary America? To what extent was colonial commerce with China hampered not only by official British limitation of the nature and quantity of goods that could be imported, but also by restriction of sea routes colonial merchants could utilize in acquiring products? What part did Americans, rather than Englishmen, play in the Colonial period in initiating China commerce? How did merchants' pre-Revolutionary experiences effect their behavior in the post-Revolutionary period?

2. What were the experiences of United States citizens in dealing with the trade, tariff, and diplomatic policies of their own government, especially during the Opium War (1839–42), when their country, for the first time, engaged in serious diplomatic and military contact with China? What role did Philadelphians play in the "hottest" commerce of the China trade—the smuggling of opium into China?

3. What was the derivative economic effect of Philadelphia's China trade on the home port, in terms of the expansion of local business in response to the requirements of the trade, and in terms of the reinvestment of China trade profits?

The issue of the opium trade gives rise to the second major issue of Philadelphia's China trade—its social significance. Of particular importance are the opinions which early Americans formulated about the Chinese as a race and as a culture. These views may have special relevance for our present-day dealings both with Asia and with Asian-American citizens of the United States. Professors Hilary Conroy and T. Scott Miyakawa recently observed, concerning Japanese-Americans, that a "racist heritage" with strong emotional overtones may have justified in the minds of many Americans the indignities and inequalities deliberately imposed on Asian immigrants and Asian Americans.[10]

A substantially larger body of historical research has been done on the attitudinal questions than on the commercial ones. These studies have scrutinized American opinion of the Chinese race and the Chinese culture. The traditional view of historians has been that until the outbreak of the Opium War in 1839, excellent business and personal relations existed between Americans and Chinese, and that for the most part Chinese were not disparaged in biological or cultural terms. Yale China specialist K. S. Latourette wrote that during these years of gradually increasing knowledge, the American opinion of China was "largely one of respect and admiration." Tyler Dennett, in his survey of the early American experience in East Asia, reported that the personal relations of the Chinese and Americans came to be "those of mutual respect and even, in many cases, of affection." Harold Isaacs, in his analysis of American images of China, argued that the early American opinion of China was one of respect, and that an "Age of Contempt" commenced only after the Opium War. Edward Graham, who made a survey of American media images of China between 1785 and 1900, concluded that the essential assumptions of media opinion were that the Chinese and American peoples had a relationship of particular friendship, that each nation had an important role to play in the development of the other, and that the process would be morally and materially advantageous to both. The anti-Oriental sentiment and discriminatory legislation which began to materialize toward the end of the nineteenth century bore no relationship to the basically good relationships engendered by the East Coast China trade before 1840. Anti-Orientalism, Graham suggested, was a phenomenon with origins in the American West, and particularly within the labor-management tensions of that region.[11]

The findings of one scholar, Stuart Creighton Miller, did not conform with this historical consensus. While conceding that some early Americans did possess a positive image of a China of "ancient greatness and hoary wisdom, the China of Confucius, Father Ricci, Leibniz, and Voltaire," Miller argued that most early Americans came to assume a highly negative opinion of a China, as a "stagnating, perverse, semi-civilized breeding ground for swarming inhuman hordes."[12] According to Miller such an image, of biological and racial inferiority, was engendered in the eighteenth and early nineteenth centuries and found its fullest expression in the United States with the 1882 passage of the Chinese Exclusion Act. That bill effectively halted Chinese immigration to the United States. Miller took issue with the explanation traditionally offered for the passage of that Act, that it was basically the result of pressures and sentiment from the West Coast, and particularly California. The evidence which he gathered led him to conclude that the anti-Chinese sentiment of the late nineteenth century was a national, not a regional phenomenon. Cultural anxiety over the admission of such an unfamiliar and dissimilar migrant as the "Chinaman" was not, according to Miller, confined to any one section of the country.[13]

Miller's thesis relates to the early China trade in that he makes the claim that the ideological input of the trade contributed to a tradition of sinophobia. While I shall not attempt to explain Oriental exclusion, we can examine whether the predominant ideological input of the China trade in one specific American region could or could not have contributed to a tradition of anti-Chinese prejudice. In doing this, the following questions will be entertained:

1. What did key individuals whose opinions were influential in early Philadelphia feel about the Chinese race and culture? Three somewhat overlapping constituencies will be examined: intellectuals, merchants who went to China, and traders who remained stateside. What impression was conveyed to a broader public through their published and unpublished commentary and their museum displays? Traditional historians have generally agreed on the nature of early American views toward two facets of Chinese culture: the Chinese government and the merchant community. With respect to the government, the historical consensus has been that there was much friction and conflict between Yankees and members of the Chinese ruling elite. On the other hand, relations between American merchants and their native Chinese counterparts were of an opposite nature. Hosea Morse, perhaps the most prolific historian of early Sino-Western relations, summarized the traditional historical view of merchant-to-merchant relations when he wrote that "there grew up side by side, during a century of joint working, a body of Chinese and foreign merchants, than whom there has never been a more honorable, with never a written contract, with many an occasion of help in time of difficulty, and with much sympathy and friendliness from one to the other."[14]

2. How were the Oriental objects and ideas, which the China trader transported to Penn's town, appraised and utilized? The importance of material culture, heretofore not included in studies of overall early American attitudes toward the Chinese, should not be overlooked. In an era before the development of photography, the depiction of China on imported paintings, porcelain, and fabric, as well as the re-creation of a Chinese environment through architecture and landscaping, helped early Americans formulate their image of the Celestial Kingdom. These visual impressions struck anyone who purchased decorated China goods or saw Chinese motifs. The image conveyed by material culture, when combined with written commentary, oral accounts, and the visual impact of museum dioramas, merged into a total formulation of an opinion of China.

We begin evaluating attitudes toward China which were held by early Philadelphians by considering intellectuals who developed a strong interest in East Asia and frequently published their researches. These men gravitated in the eighteenth and nineteenth centuries around an organization bearing the formidably self-explanatory title "American Philosophical Society Held at Philadelphia for Promoting Useful Knowledge." Approximately twenty members of this association took a serious interest in China. These "orientalists" included the organization's founder, Benjamin Franklin, whose "useful" concerns in that part of the world centered on the development of navigation, cartography, and trade; Charles Thomson, the Secretary of the Continental and U.S. Congresses, who shared with Franklin a serious interest in the development of American trade and foreign relations; Humphry Marshall, a botanist concerned with the development of American agriculture through the importation of new breeds and grafts, including some from China; APS Secretary Peter Duponceau, a student of exotic languages, including Chinese; and Andreas Van Braam and Nathan Dunn, two APS members who went to Cathay, and, upon their return, initiated publications and public displays about the land where they had resided. Robert Waln, Jr., although not an APS member, may also be included as part of the Philadelphia intellectual circle which centered on the organization. A self-educated Quaker historian of China, Waln did his research in the East, returned home, published much of it, and died at the age of thirty-one. Waln might well have received APS membership had he lived longer.

A second group of Philadelphians under examination are the seafarers who, some in the company of their families, made the trek to China. This group was composed of approximately seventy-five individuals.[15] Waln, Dunn, and Van Braam overlap into this group, although their impact may be considered as great in the realm of ideas as in the development of commerce. This second group was a hardy breed of American, intellectually dynamic, aggressive, and usually in good enough physical shape to endure a year-long voyage to China and remain in that alien, sometimes hostile, environment for extended periods of time. Some stayed ten or twenty years. Most of these people went in a managerial capacity having to do with the China trade, such as resident merchant in Canton or captain, purser, or supercargo (chief commercial agent) aboard a merchant ship. Several went as doctors. One, after a short time in business, went into journalism, inaugurating English-language newspapers, and possibly also photography, on the China coast.

In focusing on this second group, we unfortunately must exclude the largest group of individuals involved in early Sino-American relations, the merchant seamen who manned the China trade ships. Since most of these sailors were illiterate, we have no record of their comments to examine aside from "X—his mark" on crew lists. We do not even seem to have the type of behavioral evidence which Jesse Lemisch used to explain the political attitudes of American sailors during the Revolutionary period, such as the attempted prison breaks of John Paul Jones' men from English jails, or riots of Boston sailors to protest British rule.[16] Although we are compelled to look at the history of the China trade through the eyes of the wealthy, from the top down, we will attempt to see how the behavior and attitudes of wealthy and powerful individuals may have affected the broader American population.

Among the seafarers under examination, the two outstanding personalities seem to have been Benjamin Wilcocks (1776–1845) and John Latimer (1793–1865). Although both began as men of substantial means—Wilcocks as the grandson of a Pennsylvania chief justice, Latimer as the inheritor of a century of colonial farming and shipping wealth—the two achieved much in the business world in their own right. Both spent extensive periods of time as resident merchants in Canton, handling that end of Philadelphia's China trade. Wilcocks personally developed both branches of Philadelphia's China opium trade and amplified that illegal commerce during his tenure as U.S. consul in Canton. He may also have been the pioneer of opium shipment from Smyrna, Turkey, to Batavia, Indonesia. Latimer inherited and enlarged Wilcocks' opium business when Ben returned to the United States in the 1820s, thereby compounding the already considerable Latimer family fortune.

A third body of Philadelphians under examination never departed from the Quaker City because they performed the indispensable stateside tasks of financing and managing voyages. This group, composed of about seventy-five individuals, received and sold merchandise sent to them on consignment and made the crucial and usually risky managerial decisions about foreign peoples and places. These entrepreneurs digested the strange tales their agents wove into commercial correspondence and formulated opinions to be passed on to a broader American public. Apparently the two outstanding personalities of this group were Robert Morris (1735–1806) and Stephen Girard (1750–1831; see frontispiece illustration). Both pioneered new sea routes, utilized advanced maritime technology, and developed innovative managerial techniques which other Philadelphia businessmen followed. Both men's accomplishments may be considered all the more formidable when it is realized that they, unlike Wilcocks and Latimer, were of very humble immigrant origins. Morris, born in Liverpool and an emigré to Philadelphia as a child, built the basis of his fortune before and during the Revolutionary War as importer, land speculator, and lender of money to the Continental Congress. Girard, a tough, one-eyed French mariner, was stranded in Philadelphia during the American Revolution, stayed on, and developed the basis of his fortune in Atlantic and Caribbean commerce. Both entrepreneurs, after independence had been won, devoted their substantial assets and administrative talents to the initiation of a native American China trade.

This study, then, will deal with the twin issues of Philadelphia's early China trade: how commerce developed, and what attitudes evolved. Where it is logically and empirically possible, the Philadelphia experience will be compared to that of other early American seaport cities. Chapter 2 focuses on commercial, diplomatic, and attitudinal aspects of Philadelphia's China trade during the Colonial period, from the city's 1682 establishment to about 1783. Chapter 3 deals with commercial and diplomatic aspects of the port's post-Revolutionary China trade, with the exception of the opium trade. Attitudes toward the very earliest direct United States-China voyages, and toward the use of Chinese decorative household goods, will also be discussed. Chapter 4 concentrates on the commercial, diplomatic, and attitudinal history of Philadelphia's opium trade. Chapter 5 concerns post-Revolutionary intellectual attitudes toward China as reflected in published scholarship, museums, and in the utilization of Chinese agricultural and architectural technology. That chapter will also offer an overall profile of early Sino-American relations as conducted from one early American harbor town.

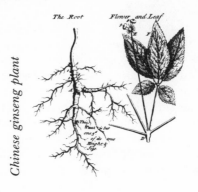

Chinese ginseng plant

The Root   Flower and Leaf

2 The Colonial Impetus 1682–1783

By introducing the produce of those countries which lie on the east side of the old world, and particularly those of China, this country may be improved beyond what heretofore might have been expected. And could we be so fortunate as to introduce the industry of the Chinese, their arts of living and improvements in husbandry, as well as their native plants, America might in time become as populous as China.
—Charles Thomson[1]

In the Colonial period, Philadelphia merchants acquired mercantile and navigational expertise that would later be useful to them in a direct China trade of their own. They assumed an intellectual predisposition favorable to direct trade with China, and became increasingly disenchanted with British mercantilist regulation of the indirect type of trade which they were obliged to conduct. Both attitudinal processes occurred gradually. Their origins may be traced as far back as the founding of the Province of Pennsylvania and City of Philadelphia in 1682. The processes reached their culmination and received their fullest expression in 1783, when American independence was recognized by the British and when Philadelphia merchants undertook the establishment of a direct China trade of their own.

A Business Community Is Formed

Prior to 1783, and to a considerable extent thereafter until at least 1846, America's international trade was conducted in the colonial fashion wherein each municipality was a discrete entity. The American business historian Thomas Cochran has noted in this respect:

> In spite of intercolonial trade in some items, each major port with its tributary back country was a separate business community remote from its neighbors. The personal ties that bound the business world together were more often between American merchants and the houses of Liverpool or London than between men on this side of the Atlantic. Business men of Charleston were more at home in London than in Boston.[2]

The economic development of Philadelphia and the growth of its merchant community were no exception. The city was founded in 1682 by English Quakers led by William Penn. A cohesive and well-capitalized merchant community developed with strong ties to the agricultural producers of the city's hinterland and to agents abroad. Ties between Philadelphia Quaker merchants and their kin abroad were a constant feature of the city's colonial and early national economic development, and facilitated the early development of a lucrative export trade in flour and lumber from the province to Europe, Canada, and the West Indies. Furthermore, the well-known Quaker policy of toleration, liberal by seventeenth-century standards, helped to populate the colony and gave it a cultural, ethnic, and mercantile vitality not seen again in America until the migrations of the nineteenth century. German farmers of numerous persecuted sects settled the city's hinterland. Jewish businessmen brought to the city of Philadelphia a network of foreign trade connections second only to that of the Quakers. By 1785, Philadelphia was not only the most populous but probably the most cosmopolitan city in the United States, with a significantly large and intellectual French emigré community, and an ethnic diversity that embraced Chinese and East Indians as well as the inhabitants of European ancestry, not to mention blacks.[3]

The economic growth of the city was fostered, in its broader aspects, by its fortune in being almost completely surrounded by grain-producing lands that an industrious populace was quick to exploit. The commercial development of the port proceeded in stages that had been the pattern for the development of English capitalism during two centuries: a progression from farming to the export of commodities, to the ownership of vessels, to the ultimate translation of profits into domestic manufacture and internal improvements. The experience of three Philadelphia mercantile families prominent in the China trade may be cited as examples of stages of this process.

The Waln family, members of George Fox's original Quaker meeting in England, joined Penn in the founding of Philadelphia in 1682. By 1772, the Walns had built their own flour mill in Walnford, Monmouth County, New Jersey. The Donnaldsons, a non-Quaker family, were, in pre-Revolutionary times, farmers, grain merchants, and manufacturers of ship bread in Montgomery County, Pennsylvania. The non-Quaker Latimer family, whose Philadelphia town house has been noted, originally emigrated from Newry, Ireland, to Pennsylvania in 1736 to become farmers near Lancaster. By mid-century, James Latimer had moved southeast to the rich grain-producing lands along Delaware's Christina River. Instead of continuing as a farmer, he purchased several flour mills and a private wharf, and was shipping both grain and flour to Philadelphia. By 1775, James was listed as one of four owners of a 170-ton Philadelphia-built-and-based merchant ship, the *Liberty*. By the time of the Revolution, all three families had expanded from purely agricultural pursuits and were using their own vessels to transport other people's grain out of the port of Philadelphia and abroad. James Latimer's grandson John, like Waln and Donnaldson kin, ultimately would expand the family's interests into East Asian trade.[4]

The experience of the three families indicates the importance of the regional commercial metropolis—Philadelphia—for people who basically resided on the periphery of the economic region, but who wished to expand from agriculture to shipping, brokerage, and large-scale finance and investment. The commercial rise of these three families, and particularly their ability to expand, diversify, and prosper within one economic region, reflected the nature of America's foreign trade up to the first half of the eighteenth century. While families did rise from farming to shipping thereafter, by the mid-eighteenth century it was also possible for newly arrived immigrants to build up fortunes exclusively through the gradual development of a merchandising and overseas shipping business. Thus, without dirtying their hands in agriculture, Robert Morris and Thomas Willing, both immigrants, built up one of the colony's most successful and best known mercantile houses. In similar fashion the Gratzes, Marxes, Levys, Ettings, and Stephen Girard all prospered.

In broadest terms, both the import and export sectors of Philadelphia's Colonial commerce demonstrated steady growth, particularly after the conclusion of the war with Spain and France in 1748, rising to peaks in 1760–62 and 1772–73.[5] Philadelphia merchants became the major, but hardly the exclusive, import and export agents for a region that remained fairly constant geographically, although settlement patterns within the region do gradually shift southwestward and westward of the metropolis. The map of the Philadelphia economic region in colonial times (see illustration) also depicts Philadelphia's commercial hinterland as late as 1846, although the growth of the port of Baltimore severed the Susquehanna basin from Philadelphia's economic sphere of influence as early as the 1780s. As far as Oriental trade is concerned, the region came to include Wilmington, which, although a port of entry, did not develop a China trade of its own.[6]

Philadelphia merchants gained, through their foreign trade, a familiarity with techniques of international business that would later be useful to them in the China trade: managing fleets; selling both wholesale and retail; and auctioneering. They stocked a few basic lines of "staple" commodities, as well as general merchandise. They maintained a constant stream of remittances both locally and abroad over long periods of time. They scrupulously studied foreign price levels, which were considered the best barometer of overseas trade conditions. They became accustomed to being paid in Europe and the West Indies in specie and bills of exchange, which were subsequently traded for commodities for the home port. They developed a shrewdness in evaluating people over great distances and in recruiting dependable captains and agents.

Intellectual Attitudes Conducive to the China Trade

Within a basic commercial context, two not altogether unrelated intellectual attitudes emerged in Colonial Philadelphia that would, each in its own way, foster the development of an American China trade. The first was the deliberate promotion by Philadelphia intellectuals of useful and practical solutions to immediate problems. Aspects of commerce with China could be rationalized in such terms. The second was a lighthearted fascination with the art objects and products of China, which offered a pleasant alternative to dominant classical modes, and which in turn had economic implications for import merchants.

The eighteenth-century intellectuals of Philadelphia were men of the Enlightenment. "Useful knowledge" was the term used by Franklin and Jefferson, both long-term Presidents of Philadelphia's American Philosophical Society, to characterize the object of their

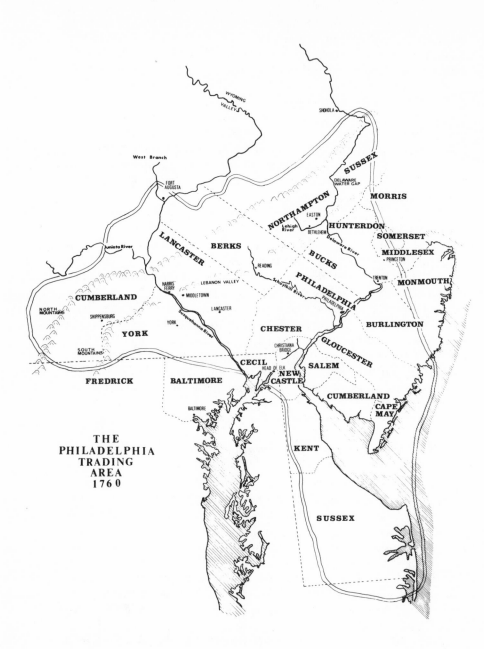

The Philadelphia Trading Area, 1760.

scholarly research. They were not concerned with metaphysics, which sought truth for its own sake. Truth was a quality revealed only when a doctrine or theory could be shown to have practical usefulness. In 1768, Charles Thomson advised the American Society Held at Philadelphia for Promoting Useful Knowledge, a predecessor society of the APS:

> Knowledge is of little use when confined to mere speculation; But when speculative truths are reduced to practice, when theories, grounded upon experiments, are applied to common purposes of life, and when, by these, agriculture is improved, trade enlarged, and the arts of living made more easy and comfortable, and, of course, the increase and happiness of mankind promoted, knowledge then becomes really useful.[7]

William Smith, a member of Thomson's circle who became the innovative Provost of the University of Pennsylvania, asserted that

> the man who will discover a method of preventing the fly from destroying turnips or who will point out a new and profitable article of agriculture and commerce will deserve more from his fellow citizens and from heaven than all the Latin and Greek scholars or all the teachers of technical learning that ever existed in any age or country.[8]

The desire of both of these men for the contrived expansion of trade and commerce found expression in the promotional activities of the APS and its predecessor societies. As early as 1768 and up through the middle of the nineteenth century, these Philadelphia organizations were involved in advancement of practical research related to China. In 1771, the first volume of the APS *Transactions* contained the following preface by Charles Thomson:

> By introducing the produce of those countries which lie on the east side of the old world, and particularly those of China, this country may be improved beyond what heretofore might have been expected. And could we be so fortunate as to introduce the industry of the Chinese, their arts of living and improvements in husbandry, as well as their native plants, America might in time become as populous as China.[9]

In particular, Thomson felt that the development of American cotton, silk, tea, and porcelain industries could be fostered through the importation of Chinese specimens and techniques. He cited the similarity in latitude and climate of Philadelphia and Peking, the similarities in vegetation, and the already successful integration of three Chinese plants—rice, whisk, and the Chinese vetch—into American agriculture. Noting the "great variety" of Pennsylvania clays, Thomson postulated that "a porcelain equal to that brought from China may be made here." In part because of the interest in China initiated by Thomson in the Colonial period, the APS, in post-Revolutionary America, actively promoted the introduction of techniques of Chinese sericulture, animal husbandry, and agriculture.[10]

Another contribution of the APS toward the development of Sino-American relations was the publication of ethnographic research which tended to downplay the ethnic and cultural gap between the two cultures. In particular, the society in 1779 published Benjamin Rush's arguments on the "common origin" of all races. Rush wrote:

> We shall render the belief of the whole human race being descended from one pair, easy, and universal, and thereby not only add weight to the Christian revelation, but remove an obstacle to the exercise of the universal benevolence which is inculcated by it.[11]

After about 1810, the ethnographic notions of Rush came under attack in Philadelphia from proponents of theories of diverse and inherently unequal origins of the races, which will be discussed later. However, prior to the emergence of this "American School" of ethnology in about 1815, the physical characteristics of the Chinese seem to have posed no major obstacle to Sino-American relations. The APS played a part in the propagation of such positive attitudes.[12]

In addition to the utilitarian notions advanced by the APS, romantic idealism also played its part in the origin of colonial commerce with China. In the seventeenth and eighteenth centuries, many Americans and Europeans entertained a fascination with the exotic. This emotion was at least partly rooted in dissatisfaction with dominant classical modes. In political and economic thought, such discontent had been expressed in the novel pragmatism of the Enlightenment. In art and in social behavior, one means of relieving the monotony of classicism was the introduction of refreshingly outlandish Chinese goods and customs. Early in the eighteenth century, the upper classes of Europe and America adopted the Chinese custom of tea drinking, together with its porcelain equipage and an elaborate set of social rites of clearly Western origin. This chic pastime was gradually adopted by the lower classes as well, leading one Philadelphia merchant to observe by the early nineteenth century that tea drinking in America had become "more incorporated with the necessaries than the luxuries of life." Other Americans enlivened classic motifs in their homes with the introduction of Chinese wallpaper, artifacts, and designs, such as those in Mayor Samuel Powel's house in Philadelphia (1765), or in Jefferson's designs for a Chinese pavilion at Monticello (1770). The popularity of exoticity, while satisfying the desire of Americans for the bizarre, had an economic effect as well, for it created a market for imported Chinese goods.[13]

The Colonial Tea Trade

The merchants of British North America were not permitted, under the terms of the 1651 Navigation Act and subsequent legislation, to sail in their own ships to the Orient. Rather, they were obliged to purchase Chinese goods on the London market, where the goods were deposited by the British East India Company. Such a system was intended to guarantee the British a continuous inflow of wealth from the colonies. It required from the Colonial merchant the payment of middleman profits which he would not have to pay had he sailed directly to China. From about 1750 on, the merchants of Colonial Philadelphia seem to have had the mercantile and navigational expertise, and the necessary capital, to embark on such direct voyages themselves, but were restrained by the bans of British mercantilist legislation.

The acquisition of mercantile skills necessary for marketing and purchasing Chinese goods came in response to Colonial demand for Chinese goods. As early as 1721, tea had come into general use in New England. By 1781, a traveler noted that most Americans drank the beverage at least twice a day. The Colonial Philadelphia merchant Samuel Wharton shipped teas across Pennsylvania to the Mohawk, Conojohare, and Delaware Indians, as well as to frontiersmen living in the Appalachians from New York to North Carolina. He wrote that it cost less than one cent/pound/mile to ship tea across Pennsylvania.[14]

British customs records kept between 1750 and 1774 attest to the large volume of tea consumed by Americans. England exported to Pennsylvania about 40,000 pounds per year, one-fifth of the average amount shipped from London to all of continental North America. Philadelphia merchants thus acquired expertise in judging and marketing the many grades of American tea long before they actually dealt directly with Chinese merchants.[15]

Colonial resistance to British taxation of tea has generally been associated with Boston patriots, but many Philadelphians put up an equally stiff opposition. They also favored less radical measures, such as compromise with, or modification of, existing British regulation.

Smuggling was the major manifestation of Philadelphia opposition to British control of the tea trade. Philadelphia merchants had developed a lucrative tea-smuggling strategy by the mid-eighteenth century. Figures are unfortunately unavailable on this clandestine commerce, but the patterns of trade and some of the techniques used were noted in mercantile correspondence. The Dutch West India Island of St. Eustacia seems to have been the purchase point for the contraband, which was then spirited into Philadelphia either by sea or overland across New Jersey. Sometimes local customs officials connived in the operation. The Dutch, being free traders, would sell to anyone willing to pay, with no questions asked.[16]

The main Philadelphia merchants who engaged in smuggling were Thomas Willing, Robert Morris, Thomas Riché, and Thomas Wharton. These men displayed in their smuggling activities as much innovation and craft as any other enterprising colonials. Willing and Wharton used old or forged excise documents to get their shipments past customs. The sender of the illegal goods marked the cases and invoiced the shipment in accord with the false papers. Customs officers were also bribed, prompting Richard Waln to comment that "our smugglers find it safest to employ those who are appointed to prevent the trade." The high point in the smuggling trade was reached in the mid-fifties. By 1757, the Philadelphia merchant John Kidd observed that "not more than 16 chests of tea legally imported from England have been consumed in Pennsylvania in two previous years, although total yearly consumption must have been ca. 200 chests."[17]

The British were hardly pleased with the clandestine traffic. Although they were ultimately powerless to end the collusion of their constabulary in America, they did make some attempts to halt it. New Jersey's vital role in the transshipment of smuggled goods was terminated by Governor Robert Hunter Morris, who conducted a vigorous campaign against this trade in 1756 and succeeded in bringing this branch of the contraband trade to a virtual halt. The Island of St. Eustacia was sacked by British troops in 1780 largely because of its notorious role in the smuggling trade to America.[18]

Although some Philadelphia merchants continued to devise new ways to smuggle tea even after Governor Morris' crackdown, others cooperated with British mercantilist regulation and even devised ways to make the system work more smoothly. Abel James, Henry Drinker, John Reynell, and Daniel Roberdeau were several of the merchants in the city who abstained from the smuggling trade. Roberdeau, who traded with the West Indies, where the temptation to engage in smuggling was greatest, wrote a firm in Curaçao that he was willing to serve them only "within limit of the laws of trade." One author has asserted that these merchants abstained because, as strict Quakers, they were particularly scrupulous about obeying all regulations.[19] While religious faith may have played some part in these merchants' abstinence, it would also seem possible that their opposition might have been economically motivated. They may have feared boycott by colleagues in America or in England if they engaged in illegal activity. Furthermore, they may have simply felt that flying in the face of the system wasn't worth the risk of official retaliation. The British mercantilist system, with all its limitations, had been the source of their past profit and could reasonably be expected to facilitate profits in the future.

Among Colonial Philadelphia merchants, Samuel Wharton was distinguished both by his abiding faith in the British mercantilist system and, at the same time, by his desire to change and improve it through existing channels. He apparently hoped that taxation upon tea would be repealed through parliamentary means. In February 1770, after a brief period of lobbying in London for parliamentary repeal, Wharton expressed the hope that "some of the *Inns* may have wisdom enough to join in the repeal of the objectionable Acts."[20] Wharton was, furthermore, astute enough to realize that mere repeal of taxation would not be incentive enough to make merchants forsake smuggling: tea had to be brought into the colonies at a cost cheaper than via St. Eustacia. He wrote:

> A repeal of the 3d. tax would not enable the American merchants to lodge money in London for the purpose of buying teas, and would not prevent them from purchasing teas at those foreign places where they can exchange flour corn & c. for them.[21]

To remedy this problem and return the tea trade to the British East India Company, Wharton suggested that a mercantilist technique be employed. The mother country should restructure the shipping regulations to America so that tea could be brought in more cheaply. He advised, first, the direct transshipment of the East India Company's teas from London to American consignees, without those teas taking on the additional cost of storage and auction sale on the London market. Second, he suggested that those teas be consigned in London "upon a credit of 9 or 12 months."[22] The provision for the extension of credit might solve the problem of merchants' having to "lay down the dollar" for London teas. Instead, they could sell their grain and flour in London on the fixed auction dates, and then pay the East India Company whatever charges had accumulated on their tea accounts over the preceding nine to twelve months. This was, essentially, the same system employed in Holland by the Dutch East India Company.

The one factor which Wharton underestimated was the depth of emotion among some Philadelphians against any revised British tea schemes, even if they could be as lucrative to Americans as the smuggling trade. When the British Board of Trade agreed to experimentation with the Wharton scheme in limited fashion in 1773, public protests were held. Wharton persevered, securing as Philadelphia consignees his own brothers, plus the loyal merchants James and Drinker and Jonathan Brown. Patriots opposed the landing of tea because the particularly hated tax on tea was still to be collected. In 1773, when the first tea ship was due in Philadelphia under the new scheme, the consignees were obliged to resign their commissions after receiving threats, public protests, and visits by committees. When the ship appeared in port, it was unable to unload its cargo and returned to England. Wharton's tea scheme, frustrated by the wrath of his own countrymen rather than by any British chicanery, was not repeated. The sentiment which had emerged on this issue found its fullest expression a very short time thereafter in the outbreak of the Revolutionary War.[23]

Thus yet another British mercantilist technique had proven to be unworkable, and in effect British power in America had suffered another setback over the issue of tea—in spite of the effort of loyal merchants to strengthen, not weaken, that power. Unlike some of their colleagues, the loyal merchants had sought their wealth under terms sanctioned by the crown. Some merchants, like Wharton, saw their own wealth and the wealth of the crown as one and inseparable, in the classic mercantilist sense.

The tea trade was not the only Colonial commerce in Chinese goods in which merchants experienced frustration with British mercantilist control. They also had difficulties in their commerce in trades which were of lesser volume.

The Colonial Porcelain Trade

The extent of the colonial importation of Chinese porcelain is difficult to gauge. Porcelain was one of the major items smuggled in from St. Eustacia and elsewhere. But even in smuggler's correspondence, porcelain is referred to as "China," with no distinction between genuine Chinese porcelain and imitation wares produced in Europe at Delft, Bow, and Worcester. Franklin referred to the first appearance of "China" in his house in about 1730, but it is unclear from his reference whether he meant genuine porcelain from China or imitation.[24] In a 1758 letter, he specified that he was sending his wife some Chinaware made at Bow and Worcester as well as "one old true China basin . . . to show the difference in workmanship."[25] The diverse assortment of porcelain shards excavated in Franklin's trash pit in Philadelphia further attests to the wide variety of porcelain types in the province in Colonial times, including many crudely or simply decorated pieces of Chinese porcelain which were the weekday dishes for many Philadelphians (see illustration). Such cheap varieties may have been imported for their value as salable ballast. The picture is further complicated when it is realized that Colonial Philadelphia was producing porcelain of its own. Indeed, the Colonial porcelain trade underwent on a small scale the process of transition from importation to domestic manufacture that would occur on a larger scale in the post-Revolutionary China trade. Kaolin had been located along the bed of White Clay Creek, south of Philadelphia. A factory was opened in Southwark, Philadelphia, which has recently been excavated. The factory managed to produce a number of first-rate porcelain wares, the first in America, before it succumbed to bankruptcy in 1771. Thus although there are no reliable statistics on the Colonial porcelain trade, the evidence of material culture attests to the existence of a multitude of porcelain types in Colonial Philadelphia, with genuine Chinese porcelain in competition with many other types.[26]

The Colonial Ginseng Trade

In addition to importing Chinese goods, Philadelphia merchants were engaged in exporting to China at least one locally produced commodity. Appalachian ginseng root was used by the Chinese as a cure-all and aphrodisiac. The octopus-shaped root, with a main stem resembling ginger or parsnip, grew wild in Manchuria and Korea. In North America it was found in the Appalachians from Quebec to Georgia, and along the valleys of the Mississippi and Ohio rivers. Until recent times ginseng did not respond to artificial cultivation.

The Chinese used five types of ginseng. The highly potent and desired variety, *aralia quinquefolia,* was abundant in North America. This variety was considered particularly efficacious on the spleen, and reportedly was selling in China as late as 1911 for 250 times its weight in silver.[27]

It is unclear when settlers in North America recognized their ginseng as the same product so highly prized by the Chinese. One historian has claimed that the Dutch shipped the root down the Hudson, thence to Amsterdam, and finally to London, where it was sold to the East India Company at a 500-percent profit. This would have had to occur before the Dutch departure from Fort Orange in 1664. The veracity of the claim cannot be tested because the author did not cite his source of information.[28]

There is evidence that the Jesuits, harbingers of so much Sino-Western contact, noted early in the eighteenth century that *"ginseng de Tartarie"* was growing in North America. A Jesuit named Jartoux, while engaged in mapping Manchuria for the Chinese in 1709, made a drawing of Manchurian ginseng that was subsequently published in Paris (see illustration). Another Jesuit, Joseph Lafitau, published a memoir in Paris in 1718 which asserted that he had found that same type of ginseng growing wild in Canada. Sometime shortly after these discoveries, France opened up a lucrative trade in American ginseng to China.[29]

In 1738, the *Pennsylvania Gazette* announced its "pleasure to acquaint the world, that the famous Chinese plant ginseng is now discovered in the province, near Susquehanna."[30] By 1752, a modest trade in the drug seems to have developed between Philadelphia and London. The Philadelphia merchant James Pemberton wrote of the "great noise about the price of ginseng in London, by which some few who have shipped small parcels in the summer have obtained a very advantageous price." He expressed the hope that if the prices remained high "it will be a very profitable & beneficent thing to this part of the world."[31] It is unclear just how much ginseng was shipped from Philadelphia, as available statistics lump together ginseng shipped from all of British North America. In 1770, some 74,000 pounds of American ginseng reached London. By 1772, the drug disappeared entirely from the list of exports to England, only to reemerge in 1783 in the single shipment of several barrels of ginseng to England by one Philadelphia merchant. The drug does not appear to have sustained the steady and lucrative remittances that the Pembertons hoped for.[32]

Disenchantment with British Mercantilism

Even in the limited fashion in which Colonial Philadelphia merchants had engaged in Oriental commerce, the experience had not been an altogether successful one. In the Colonial tea trade, perhaps more than any other single line of Asiatic commerce, merchants demonstrated their dissatisfaction with British regulation by violent opposition to the landing of East India Company teas and by smuggling, which was also employed in the importation of porcelain. The hopes of the Pembertons for a large colonial ginseng trade did not materialize, nor did the hopes of Samuel Wharton for improved tea trading.

One final episode illustrated some of the difficulties between colony and mother country over the issue of Asian commerce. In 1751, 1753, and 1754, Franklin, the province's leading intellectual, and William Allen, perhaps its wealthiest merchant, sent a ship of their own in search of a Northwest Passage to China. The venture of the *Argo*, Captain Swain, immediately produced conflicts with London authorities, who questioned the propriety of the Colonial venture. Had such a route been opened by the Colonials, and commerce initiated, it would have been in violation of practically every Navigation Act. Furthermore, Allen held definite intentions in terms of striking "a lucrative trade on the coast of Labrador," in case the search for the Passage proved fruitless. A London-based "Northwest Company" had already applied to the Board of Trade for a monopoly of the Labrador trade, which, if granted, would have made the Colonial venture futile. There were also jurisdictional quarrels with the Hudson's Bay Company, whose charter had already been granted. The disputes were only laid to rest when the *Argo* returned to Philadelphia in 1754, at the end of its third and final attempt, having neither located a Northwest Passage to China nor established a Labrador trade. It would be another thirty years before Philadelphia merchants would again seriously entertain the prospect of direct trade with China.[33]

Chinese cotton plant

3 The Mercantile Response

For us, the Indian Looms are free,
And Java strips her spicy tree.

—Philip Freneau[1]

After 1783 Philadelphia merchants used the mercantile and navigational expertise acquired in the Colonial period to engage in direct trade with China and satisfy a popular demand for Chinese products that had also arisen in the Colonial period. This commerce was facilitated by a generally hospitable diplomatic milieu, in particular with Britain, along the sea lanes and territories between the United States and China and by the demonstration, through pioneering voyages, of the feasibility and profitability of regular commerce.

A Hospitable Diplomatic Milieu

After the conclusion of peace between Britain and the United States in 1783, subsequent relations between the two nations were conducive to the establishment of a direct American China trade. Even before the ratification of the first Anglo-American commercial treaty in 1795 (Jay's Treaty), Britain had adopted a *de facto* policy of toleration of American shipping in Asiatic and Indian Ocean ports. Jay's Treaty codified the policy of "friendly toleration," guaranteeing the hospitable reception of American vessels in the key British ports en route to China: in St. Helena, South Africa, the Indian Ocean, India, and the Straits Settlements. In these ports, types of trade regulation were instituted which had distinct commercial advantages for both Britain and the United States. From the British viewpoint, tariffs could be levied on most American commerce, while those avenues of American trade which represented a threat to British interests could be restricted or eliminated entirely, in classic mercantilist fashion. From the American viewpoint, ships had safe havens. Thus, for example, when the Philadelphia ship *United States* entered Indian waters in 1784, it was accorded a cordial reception by the British authorities. Yet the *United States* and subsequent American ships were restricted on the export of Indian saltpeter, an essential ingredient in gunpowder, and on the eastward shipment of opium, a commodity which English merchants were profitably exporting to China, and which they were reluctant to relinquish to traders of other nations. From the British viewpoint, the granting of safe havens to American ships had the additional function of providing backup shipping facilities that could be utilized in the event of the incapacitation of British Asiatic shipping, as occurred during both the Napoleonic and Opium Wars.

At the same time that Britain made known her toleration of American Asiatic shipping, she demonstrated unrelenting hostility toward the traditional American trade with her West Indian colonies, which she wished to reserve for imperial shipping. After the recommencement of Anglo-French hostilities in 1793, American neutral shipping with French West Indian colonies was regularly harassed by Britain. In that year alone, Britain seized over three hundred American ships trading with the French West Indies. Many American merchants who had made the basis of their fortunes in West Indian shipping, like Morris and Girard, were reluctant to relinquish their lucrative trade, despite British chastisement. Girard went so far as to furnish his ships with duplicate sets of documents: a genuine set, which revealed trade with French islands; and a spurious set, which showed no such commerce. The Jay Treaty, after much diplomatic and Congressional wrangling, was mute on the key questions of American West Indian trade and American neutral rights. The agreement did somewhat stabilize American trade with England, which, as early as 1789, had surpassed all prewar tonnage levels; and contained the aforementioned favorable provisions for American trade with Asia.[2]

Robert Morris' "Native Oak": Philadelphia Merchants and the First United States-China Voyage

Britain's manifestation of diplomatic toleration of an American presence in the Orient was not sufficient in itself to induce American merchants to embark on their own Asian voyages. Some clue as to the commercial feasibility of American-Oriental commerce was also needed. In this respect, Britain also was to provide assistance. Help came in the form of the imperially sponsored discoveries of Captain James Cook, on his 1776 Pacific venture. Cook attempted to locate a Northwest Passage to China by sailing up the Pacific, rather than the Atlantic, coast of North America. The voyage was followed with keen interest in Philadelphia, particularly by Franklin, organizer of his own unsuccessful Northwest expeditions. While the voyage was in progress, during the height of the American Revolution, Franklin secured a military order forbidding American naval interference with Cook's trip, due to its extraordinary navigational and commercial importance. Among several reports of the voyage that reached Philadelphia by the early 1780s were Lieutenant John Rickman's account, published in London in 1781 and in Philadelphia in 1783, and Seaman John Ledyard's account, printed in Hartford in that same year. Two vital pieces of information emerged from these volumes. A Northwest Passage had not been found from the Pacific side. If Oriental commerce was to be prosecuted at all, the traditional routes around Cape Horn and the Cape of Good Hope would have to be utilized. Shortcuts via Labrador or the Pacific Northwest were not navigationally feasible. The second piece of information was that fur pelts, secured from Indians of the Northwest Coast for practically no money at all, fetched extraordinary prices from Chinese merchants in Canton. A profitable trade might be undertaken shipping these goods across the Pacific, and then taking on China goods for American or European markets.[3]

John Ledyard was apparently one of the few Americans on Cook's trip. On his return to the United States in 1783, he circularized the major merchants of the United States in an attempt to find underwriters for a Pacific Northwest fur voyage. In May of 1783, Morris of Philadelphia took an interest in his scheme. Morris had a propensity for unconventional business practices and was also sadly aware of the ongoing uncertainties in Philadelphia's traditional Atlantic and Caribbean commerce. However, in Morris' efforts to secure other underwriters to share the risk of such a voyage, he ran into difficulties because of the equally great uncertainty of Northwest Coast navigation. A partnership was finally struck between Morris, William Duer of Philadelphia, and Daniel Parker and John Holker of New York, with a joint capitalization of $120,000. The ship was to carry ginseng as its main cargo, along with some specie, and locally secured furs, avoiding the need for a Northwest Coast passage. The main impetus for sending a large ginseng cargo appar-

ently came early in 1784, when the Boston sloop *Harriet,* sent to
China with ginseng in December 1783, returned to the United States
with news that its ginseng had been exchanged for tea at the unusu-
ally favorable rate of two pounds for one. Even more unusual was
the fact that the *Harriet* never reached China. The exchange had
occurred at the Cape of Good Hope, between the sloop's captain and
the captain of a British East India Company vessel, who sensed the
ginseng's value, and who was perhaps a bit startled at the possibility
of American competition.[4]

The preparations for Morris' voyage took on national dimensions. A 360-ton Baltimore-built vessel was secured and christened
The Empress of China (see cover illustration). In New York, a cargo
was loaded consisting of thirty tons of Appalachian ginseng, 2,600
furs, and the remainder of the freight in specie, pig lead, and
woolen cloth. Revolutionary War expertise was drawn upon in the
selection of the captain, John Green of Philadelphia, recently re-
lieved of naval duties, and the choice of business agent or supercargo, Samuel Shaw, recently aide-de-camp of General Henry Knox.
Morris, in a grandiose gesture, wrote Secretary of State John Jay
that he was "sending some ships to China in order to encourage
others in the adventurous pursuit of commerce." Morris himself
remained in Philadelphia to plan additional voyages and manage
other enterprises. As a final, perhaps auspicious, preparation, the
ship's departure from New York was arranged for Washington's
Birthday, February 22, 1784.[5]

The unusual preparations for the *Empress* voyage were matched
by an equally unprecedented reception in Canton (see map of Can-
ton-Macao-Hong Kong). The trading conditions which the first
United States ship encountered in China were unlike any that
Americans were accustomed to in any other port of the world, with
the possible exception of the Colonial American dealings with the
East India Company monopoly. In the mid-eighteenth century, the
Chinese export merchants of Canton had joined an association in
order to monopolize Western trade. The organization then won
official government sanction of its monopoly, after paying heavy
bribes to the court. It took the name *kung-hang,* "officially authorized
guild." Westerners came to refer to this organization by its pidgin
English title, "cohong," and its members as "hong" merchants. In
1784, it was the only Chinese trading organization Western seafarers
could trade with, and only in certain staple commodities. The cohong was always willing to accept payment in specie and also accepted ginseng, furs, and rice (which could be imported duty-free).
The cohong would willingly trade with ships of any Western nation,

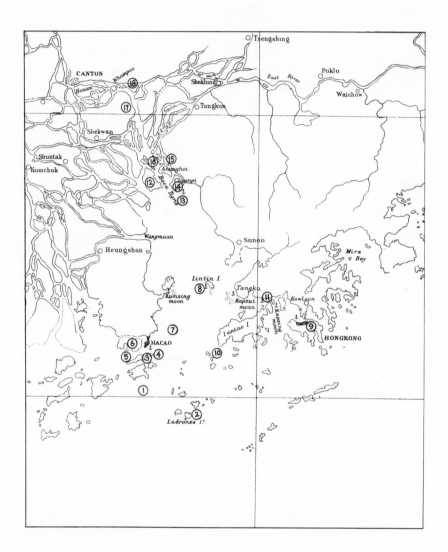

Canton-Macao-Hongkong. (See opposite for key)

so long as duties were paid, no contraband introduced, and, most important, no contact made with Chinese other than members of the cohong and the Customs Service. The Canton trade was carried out wholly without the sanction of diplomacy. There were no official relations between China and any Western states except Russia, which engaged in an overland, treaty-regulated trade with China and rarely sent ships to Canton.[6]

These conditions were largely unknown to the promoters of the *Empress* voyage. Morris was unaware, for example, of the Chinese willingness to trade with all comers and was under the mistaken impression that a foreign vessel would be permitted to trade only after its captain had produced a suitable letter of introduction from

---

The dangers that a ship in the early China Trade had overcome in its six-month voyage did not end simply because it had reached the approaches to Whampoa. Most of the typhoons, hurricanes, pirates and mutinies were behind him, but the Captain still had to contend with the monsoons, shoals and bars of the Canton (or Pearl) River. To some extent he even had to contend with his own pilot, for if current accounts are credible, there were those among the pilots whose knowledge was minimal. Frequently, it has been said, a pilot would stand on deck shouting out a steady stream of "Ports" and "Starboards" or "Steadys" thus thoroughly confusing the man at the wheel.

Nevertheless, the passage was to be negotiated, and there were several typical routes to be followed. Coming in from the South, a ship usually followed the Great Western Passage (1), the channel to the west of the Great Ladrone (2), which was the outermost island fronting the entrance to the river and which was used as a landfall for ships arriving from the south. When stopping at Macao, a ship could anchor in foul weather at the Typa Anchorage (3) between the west end of Typa Island (4) and the east end of Macarera Island (5), which always afforded secure shelter, or at the Inner Harbor between the peninsula and Patera Island (6).

The ship then entered into Macao Roads (7) and on to Lintin ("The Orphan") Island (8) about 70 miles south of Canton. There was an anchorage there about 1½ miles from the sandy beach on the southwest side. [If coming from Hong Kong (9), a ship might choose to come through the Lantao Passage to the south of Lantao Island (10), an island about 14 miles long and 5½ miles wide. Alternately he could go to the north of Lantao through Cap-sing-moon (11) (or Kap-sui-moon, "fast-water-passage").]

From Lintin Island, the ship headed north toward Lamkeet ("dragon cave," 12), just to the north of which were two rocks marking the beginning of the Bocca Tigris (or Tiger's Mouth, 13).

As the ship entered the Bocca Tigris, he was at the entrance to the Canton River. His landmarks were from that point Chuen-Pe (14), Anung Hoy "Woman's Slipper," (15), and then Tiger Island (16). From there he crossed the "Small Bar" 4¾ miles north of Tiger Island, then the Second Bar where one could see the Second Bar Pagoda (17) and seven miles farther along to the First Bar (18). From that point, says the pilot, "When Whampoa Pagoda is seen clear to the northwards, steer through Cambridge Reach, borrowing towards the North Shore."

the United States government. Captain Green had acquired such a document from Charles Thomson, then Secretary of the United States Congress, whose previous interest in China has been noted. In spite of these unknowns and uncertainties, the vast quantity of ginseng which the *Empress* brought secured it an immediate and hospitable reception in Canton. Thomas Randall, the assistant supercargo, wrote that the *Empress* unloaded "the largest quantity of ginseng ever brought to the Chinese market, more than all the British and Portuguese ships had brought for the year 1784."[7]

A return cargo was then taken on for the home market. The bulk of the return freight consisted of teas: souchong, bohea, hyson, gunpowder, and hyson skin (see illustration of tea crate). Other general sale items included six hundred silk women's gloves, silk yard goods, cotton fabrics including nankeen cloth, and Chinese cinnamon and porcelain (see illustrations of fabric samples and porcelain). Among the more unusual items in the cargo was an entire set of home furnishings crafted by Canton artisans for Robert Morris. The order included over one hundred dollars worth of hand-painted wallpaper and paper borders; four lacquered fans and a dressing box for Mrs. Morris; a glass specially decorated for that box by one "Puqua, painter on glass"; a case of procelain; and bundles of mounted silk window blinds with bamboo ribs. Despite the inclusion of isolated Chinese effects in Colonial American homes, this shipment to Morris represents the largest single order of Chinese household furnishings ever placed by an American up to that time.

On the *Empress'* return to New York in May 1785, the boat's general sale items were disposed of, netting the owners a profit of $30,000, an extraordinary 25-percent gain on their original investment. The vessel was readied for a return passage to Canton. That voyage, in addition to being commercially successful in standard China-trade items, brought back as unusual an assortment of decorative items as did the first passages. Invoices of the return cargo of the second voyage reveal, as its single most outstanding specimen, an eighty-five dollar silver tea chest, crafted by Tuhopp. This object may be the earliest Chinese export silver item for the American market, the first instance of a type of East Asian craftsmanship that became increasingly desired by wealthy Americans. The ship also carried sixty-six paper and silk fans, and twenty-four mother-of-pearl mounted fans. In this latter group, fashioned by Tackyen, may have been the fan bearing what seems to be the only known picture of the *Empress of China*.[8]

Before focusing on additional voyages to Canton that were inspired by Morris' venture, it might be well to note the impact of the

Empress on the formulation of early American ideas about China. In private correspondence, newspaper articles, and books, two themes emerged that would be echoed down to the end of Philadelphia's old China trade: the China trade was of unprecedented economic importance for the new nation; and because of that great commercial value, the Chinese people as a whole were to be held in esteem. Like Thomson's colonial view of the utilitarian nature of Chinese agriculture, these post-Revolutionary opinions were pragmatic in their motivation and very positive. Several distinct examples of early post-Revolutionary opinion may be offered.

In private correspondence about Morris' experiment, commentators came to see the Chinese people in terms which were overwhelmingly positive, perhaps to the point of being idealized. Swift, the *Empress'* purser, wrote his father in Philadelphia that "although the Chinese had never heard of us, they appear perfectly to understand and wish the importance and necessity of a trade here to the advantage of both nations."[9] Supercargo Samuel Shaw confided that "when, by the map, we conveyed to them an idea of the extent of our country, with its present and increasing population, they were not a little pleased at the prospect of so considerable a market for the productions of their own empire." Such sentiment quickly spread beyond those directly connected with the voyage. Ten days after the *Empress'* return to America in May 1785, Congressman Richard Henry Lee expressed the view that the Chinese were "glad to see a new source of commerce opened to them from a new people."[10]

Such privately expressed desires for a Sino-American friendship bolstered by extensive trade also emerged in the media. Newspaper accounts of the *Empress'* unprecedented commercial success appeared up and down the East Coast almost immediately upon that ship's return in May 1785. In what was perhaps a typical American newspaper exultation on the commercial significance of Morris' venture, Boston's *Massachusetts Centinel,* of May 18, 1785, editorialized that "this passage is one of the greatest nautical prodigies we ever recollect hearing."[11] Philadelphia's *Pennsylvania Packet,* of May 16, 1785, made the slightly more subdued observation that Americans would no longer have to import China goods via Europe:

> As the ship has returned with a full cargo, and of such articles as we generally import from Europe, it presages a happy period of our being able to dispense with that burdensome traffic which we have heretofore carried onto the prejudice of our rising empire.[12]

Apparently the most lyrical interpretation of the voyage's economic importance was the envoi to the *Empress* offered by the bard of the American Revolution, the New Jersey poet Philip Freneau. His commemorative piece, "On the First American Ship That Explored the Route to China and the East-Indies, After the Revolution," was published by a New York newspaper at the time of the *Empress'* departure and was reissued in book form in Monmouth, New Jersey, in 1795. It is reproduced here in its entirety:

> With clearance from Bellona won
> She spreads her wings to meet the Sun,
> Those golden regions to explore
> Where George forbade to sail before.
>
> Thus, grown to strength, the bird of Jove,
> Impatient, quits his native grove,
> With eyes of fire, and lightning's force
> Through the blue aether holds his course.
>
> No foreign tars here allow'd
> To mingle with her chosen crowd,
> Who, when return'd, might, boasting, say
> They show'd our native oak the way.
>
> To that old track no more confin'd,
> By Britain's jealous court assign'd,
> She round the stormy Cape shall sail
> And eastward, catch the odorous gale.
>
> To countries plac'd in burning climes
> And islands of remotest times
> She now her eager course explores,
> And soon shall greet Chinesian shores.
>
> From thence their fragrant TEAS to bring
> Without the leave of Britain's king;
> and PORCELAIN WARE, enchas'd in gold,
> The product of that finer mould.
>
> Thus commerce to our world conveys
> All that the varying taste can please:
> For us, the Indian looms are free,
> And Java strips her spicy tree.
>
> Great pile proceed!—and o'er the brine
> May every prosperous gale be thine,
> 'Till, freighted deep with eastern gems,
> You reach again your native streams.[13]

As in much of the other commentary, Freneau emphasized the themes of America's political and economic independence. The ship was likened to the American eagle ("bird of Jove"), which had been given clearance to sail by Bellona, the goddess of war. Americans now sailed where "George forbade" to sail before and without leave of Britain's "jealous court." According to Freneau, no "foreign tars" were allowed on the voyage, lest they claim credit for it. Americans were no longer confined to that old "track," by which he apparently meant the highly restricted transatlantic trade routes of the Colonial period, but could directly purchase from China such delectable items as fragrant teas and porcelain, both products previously the monopoly of the British East India Company. Freneau noted that China could produce porcelain that was "the product of that finer mould," an apparent reference to the superior quality of Chinese export ware over that imitated in the West. He expressed the hope that porcelain encased in gold—also known as ormolu ware—would be exported from China to the United States. This product, however, down to the end of the old China trade, rarely, if ever, was listed among the exotic shipments out of Canton to America. The fact that Freneau included such a prized and expensive item among the "eastern gems" he would have liked to have seen aboard America's "native oak" is further indication of his optimism regarding the prospects of the China trade.

Samuel Shaw also assisted the development of a positive media image of China. After his return in 1785, he helped to sustain the strong and well-organized appeal to develop the China trade which Ledyard and Morris had initiated. In 1787, Mathew Carey's *American Museum*—perhaps the foremost American forum for foreign policy ideas—reprinted a letter from Shaw to Jay describing the "very indulgent" treatment the Americans had received. In 1790, the *Museum* published Shaw's "Remarks on the Commerce of America with China," which mentioned the potential of the ginseng trade—a theme stressed in additional Shaw correspondence with Jay.[14] The faith these men expressed in both an idyllic Sino-American friendship, as well as the vast potential for trade, particularly in ginseng, both came to be tempered into somewhat more realistic expectations in time. On the most basic level, however, what they and other commentators were doing was reemphasizing the twin concepts of the economic importance of the China trade to America, and esteem for the industrious Chinese race. Neither theme was original in that each had been publicized for at least sixteen years by the APS. The impact of media commentary on the *Empress* voyage, therefore, was to reinforce these two extant themes in the public mind. The additional effect of such commentary was, in immediate terms, to greatly stimulate Sino-American commerce.

Subsequent Pioneering Voyages from Philadelphia to Canton

The *Empress'* financial success, coupled with the expertise that had been gained and the strong public appeal to develop an American China trade, helped to induce Morris and others to send out additional China voyages. Between 1784 and 1804, as many as seven ships a year went from Philadelphia to China, and as many as thirty-one per year from the entire United States. After 1804, until the end of the old China trade in 1846, the number of American voyages leveled off at about thirty or forty per annum, with Philadelphia ships comprising about one-third of these passages.[15]

Voyages from Philadelphia to China were usually financed by merchants of established means sending out their own ships on their own account or by investors of smaller means pooling their resources into consortia. In both cases, after about 1792, some of the formidable problems of these distant trips were eased when financing was facilitated by insurance companies. While the actual outfitting of the vessel was expensive, the acquisition of large amounts of hard cash was a particularly vexing problem. Traditionally, such cash could be acquired through the exchange of agricultural produce of the Philadelphia region in Europe. The insurance companies eased the process in some cases by lending money "on respondentia" to China traders. Large sums were directly advanced for the purchase of specie, which was then exchanged in China for Chinese goods. After the goods were sold in the West, the insurance companies were repaid principal plus interest.[16]

Between 1784 and 1788, four voyages were sent from Philadelphia to China that were second only to the *Empress* in their commercial importance. They were the voyages of the ships *Alliance, United States, Canton,* and *Asia.* The *Alliance,* a refurbished Revolutionary War frigate, was purchased and sent out by Morris wholly on his own account. He was the first American merchant to finance a China voyage singlehandedly and established yet another trend in the China trade that other Phildelphia merchants followed. He enjoyed a managerial latitude which he had not known on the *Empress* venture, and on this occasion routed his boat via the Pacific. The ship skirted the Southern Australian coast and sailed up through the Solomons, where two previously unknown islands were named "Alliance" and "Morris." When the vessel reached Canton, after an arduous passage, the ebullient sailors commissioned a portrait of themselves from a Chinese painter on glass (see illustration). While the ship was away at sea, Morris overcommitted himself in other speculation. The timely return of the *Alliance* to Philadelphia in September 1788 redeemed Morris from the imminent threat of bankruptcy, a plague to which this entrepreneur ultimately succumbed.[17]

Other merchants, both of established wealth and of small means, continued to employ the traditional financial technique of pooling their resources and sponsoring corporate voyages. Several friends of Morris underwrote the voyage of the ship *United States* out of Philadelphia one month after the *Empress'* departure from New York. Although destined for China, the *United States* never got that far owing to difficulties aboard ship. She did initiate Philadelphia and United States trade with India and with the pepper port of Acheen, Sumatra.[18] In 1785, a consortium of six Philadelphia investors sponsored the first completed Philadelphia-Canton passage, that of the ship *Canton*, Thomas Truxtun, Master. The ship carried ginseng and specie, and made two round trips between Philadelphia and Canton.[19] In December 1787, a consortium of seventeen Philadelphia investors underwrote the voyage of the first Philadelphia-built ship to enter the China trade, the 292-ton *Asia*, Captain John Barry. Morris participated in this voyage as well. He shipped thirty casks of brandy, augmenting an ordinary ginseng and specie cargo.

The voyage of the *Asia*, out of Philadelphia, was apparently the first China venture to which Philadelphia merchant Stephen Girard chose to subscribe. After the successful return of the *Asia*, Girard made the decision to commit large blocks of his funds to Asiatic commerce. While trade with the West Indies was his major maritime activity in the years 1789–93, from 1794 on, with the exception of 1799, his West Indian trade was superseded by his growing Asiatic, European, and Latin American commerce. In 1795, Girard issued the first of four commissions to Kensington shipyards for vessels specifically suited for the China trade. The four were christened *Voltaire, Rousseau, Montesquieu,* and *Helvetius,* giving some indication of whom this practical merchant considered as his lucky patrons. Girard-owned ships made some nineteen voyages to Canton between 1798 and 1826.[20]

Girard's substantial entry into the China trade seems to mark, for Philadelphia, the end of the period of great risk in the China trade. China voyages which followed the *Asia*'s tended to be considered ordinary mercantile propositions, with risks on a par, for example, with those of Philadelphia's transatlantic trade. With the exception of the opium-trading voyages which Philadelphia merchants initiated in the nineteenth century, the luster of innovation and exploration pretty much vanished from Philadelphia's China trade after 1800.

Government Assistance through Favorable Tariff Legislation

In addition to the financial resources and expertise of the merchants themselves, Philadelphia's early Oriental trade was greatly facilitated by governmental enactment of tariff provisions favorable to such commerce. Pennsylvania tariff legislation prior to 1789 had the effect of confining the China trade to vessels owned and built in the United States—thereby stimulating a native American China trade. After 1787, for example, tea could be imported duty-free in American ships coming directly from east of the Cape of Good Hope. All other vessels had to pay a tea tariff, which was raised in 1787.

When the power to levy tariffs on foreign imports passed to the Federal government in 1789, the same types of provisions were maintained as in the Pennsylvania legislation, and with the same salutary effects for the American China trade. The First Tariff Act of 1789, according to Philadelphia observer Mathew Carey, "secured to the tonnage of our merchants a monopoly of the whole (American) China trade, and gave them paramount advantages in all the other foreign trade."[21] In 1790, when duties on teas brought to the United States in American vessels were equalized somewhat with duties on teas brought in foreign vessels, there was a great uproar from the China merchants. The next year, legislation favored them, by allowing them to postpone payment of duties on teas through a bonding process. From 1791 to 1816, no new general schedule was adopted, and even though duties were gradually increased, a discrimination was still kept in favor of goods brought in American ships directly from Canton.

The desired growth of the merchant marine, the overall object of the tariff legislation, was apparent by 1794. In 1789, the American merchant marine carried only 17.5 percent of the imports and 30 percent of the exports of the United States; five years later the percentages had risen to 90 and 88 percent respectively. These figures declined during the War of 1812 (as did most American trade), but by 1820, they were back to 90 and 88 percent. After 1815, with the merchant marine out of its infancy, the China trade became increasingly taxed and was a valuable earner of revenue for the government.[22]

As Philadelphia China traders enlarged their commerce, Philadelphia was affected in two principal ways. First, Chinese art objects, handicrafts, and designs appeared with increasing frequency and abundance in the region. Second, profits generated in China commerce were rechanneled into other enterprises of regional importance.

Houqua (subtitled "Engraved by J. Sartain from the original by Chinery for B.C. Wilcocks Esq."). Houqua was a Canton merchant who traded with Wilcocks, Girard, and other Philadelphians. Mezzotint engraving. Philadelphia, undated.

Common blue-and-white porcelain bowl. Chinese, excavated in 1750 context at Front and Pine streets, Philadelphia, and restored.

Common tea crate of wood and metal. The box is inscribed PHILADᴬ Nº 134 DOROTHEA DOUGHERTY HYSON SKIN 60B W BACHE APRIL 1810. Chinese, 1810.

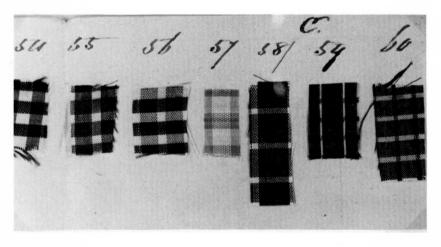

Mounted silk samples from the Canton merchant Eshing. Many of these patterns were also available in less expensive cotton fabric. Chinese, about 1819.

Custom-made punch bowl. Decorated with a drawing of Pennsylvania Hospital, and with a view of the Delaware River on the opposite side of the bowl, both in polychrome. Two unidentified English views between these two are in sepia. Given to the Board of Managers of the hospital, April 26, 1802, by Joseph Saunders Lewis. Chinese, about 1802.

Monogrammed porcelain bowl, custom-made for Stephen Girard. Grapevine medallion decoration in gold surrounds initials S.G. Chinese, about 1810.

Armorial porcelain mug, custom-made for the Penn family, bearing their coat of arms. Chinese, eighteenth century.

Examples of the use of
Pennsylvania motifs
by Chinese porcelain painters.

The Ship *Montesquieu,* by the Painter of "The Wreck of the President Adams." Stephen Girard's personal portrait of his China packet ship. Oil, canvas on wood. Chinese, about 1810.

The Crew of the *Alliance* in Canton. The *Alliance* was owned by Robert Morris of Philadelphia. The inclusion of the languid female may be a figment of the painter's imagination, since foreign women were banned from Canton at this time. Oil on glass. Chinese, about 1788.

Lacquered tea chest with inlaid mother-of-pearl and brass bat-shaped escutcheons. A gift to Stephen Girard, possibly from the Canton merchant Namsching. Chinese, about 1815.

The Importation of Chinese Decorative Goods to Post-Revolutionary Philadelphia

After 1783, Philadelphia merchants increased both the quantity and variety of Chinese goods brought into the port. Tea, silks, and nankeen cotton cloth were the staple imports from China. Chinese porcelain annually averaged only about 1 percent of the dollar value of freight imported from China up to 1839. All other Chinese imports taken together constituted an even smaller percentage than porcelain.[23] In spite of the small overall economic performance of Chinese art objects relative to the staple Sino-American trade, they had social significance; they, more than tea or plain fabric, were the "presence" of China in the early American home.

Two types of wares were ordered at Canton by Americans: custom-designed objects whose motifs had been drawn up by Westerners; and items of distinctly Oriental pattern. In each case, Westerners had the opportunity to procure goods of unusual quality and practicality at a lower production cost than for the same product in the West.[24]

In the category of custom-designed objects, porcelain was the largest single item, in terms of quantity, that was specially fashioned by the Chinese with Philadelphia designs. Philadelphians utilized the talents of Cantonese porcelain decorators to have the likenesses of familiar boats, buildings, people, landscapes, monograms, and coats of arms permanently emblazoned on clay. Two Philadelphia motifs that have been much duplicated are "Cow China" and the "Martha Washington States Plate." The first type, depicting a pastoral scene sketched in black on a white background, originated in the sketches of Mary Hollingsworth Morris. About 1800, they were taken to Canton by her brother Henry Hollingsworth and there transferred onto porcelain. The multicolor "States Plate," in the White House collection, bore Martha Washington's initials and the names of fifteen states. The cake plate, along with other porcelain pieces, was commissioned in Canton and presented to Martha Washington by the Philadelphia trader Andreas Van Braam. Plates, bowls, and sauceboats made in Canton for the Philadelphia market bore likenesses of Pennsylvania Hospital, of Morris' ship *Alliance,* and of the steamboat *Philadelphia.* Familiar pictures of Washington and Washington's Tomb were transferred onto chinaware along with the Philadelphia owners' identifying ciphers. Porcelain bore the names, crests, or initials of such Philadelphians as Penn, Wilcocks, Hayes, Girard, Waln, Barry, Thomson, McKean, Ross, Latimer, Tilghman, Cooper, and Smith. A china tray and cup carried the coat of arms of the State of Pennsylvania (see porcelain illustrations).[25]

Philadelphians also took advantage of Chinese expertise in painting on canvas or glass in a semi-Western style. Some of the Chinese artists were trained by the English painter George Chinnery (1774–1852), who lived in Canton and engaged in a lucrative practice of his own. He has been considered the artist who, in 1825, produced the portrait of the Hong merchant Houqua, which Benjamin Wilcocks brought to Philadelphia in 1827, and which was subsequently copied by the Philadelphia mezzotint engraver John Sartain (see illustration). Other Cantonese limners who worked for Philadelphians were Sunqua, who painted a portrait of the ship *Stephen Girard,* and "Spoilum," who made two calling-card portraits which Chinese merchants sent to Girard in about 1815. These were prominently displayed by Girard, who also exhibited a Chinese portrait of his ship *Montesquieu,* attributed to the same artist who painted "The Wreck of the *President Adams.*" In addition to these pictures of known provenance, Philadelphia merchants engaged unidentified Chinese artists to paint likenesses of the crew of the *Alliance,* of Van Braam's family, of Benjamin Wilcocks, of Sandwith Drinker's warehouse, and of innumerable Chinese waterfront scenes (see painting illustrations).[26]

Chinese expertise in forgery was utilized by Captain John E. Sword of Philadelphia in 1800. Sword had copies made in Canton by an unknown Chinese artist or artists of Gilbert Stuart's "Athenaeum" portrait of Washington. When these duplicates went on sale in Philadelphia in 1802, Stuart secured an injunction against their dissemination, but only after many fine examples had already been sold.[27]

The second category of decorative items shipped into post-Revolutionary Philadelphia were those objects of traditional Chinese motif which bore no Western-specified design or ornamentation. Chinese artisans were adept at producing designs of their own, many of which were subsequently copied in the West. Examples of the more exotic varieties of such items imported to Philadelphia include Sandwith Drinker's carved chairs and dressing stand, draperies in Joseph Powel's West Philadelphia estate, James Biddle's lacquered table, and John Barry's bamboo chair. Cheaper products included varieties of Canton floor and furniture mats, a straw or rattan weave that was available in many sizes and types and in three colors. These were imported to Philadelphia by Robert Morris, who sold some to Washington in 1789, and were also frequently shipped to Philadelphia by John Latimer in the early nineteenth century. Standard-issue porcelain, and particularly blue-and-white, either borderless or with "Canton" or "Nanking" edging, was the single largest traditional Chinese decorative item which the average American could afford (see illustrations). Other Chinese household items in use in Philadelphia included toys, games, and a wide variety of mass-produced fans.[28]

As the tides of taste shifted in early America, custom-made export ware was variously more and less favored by the buying public than traditional Chinese decoration. Many boats, from the *Empress of China* on, brought back both types of wares to satisfy varying tastes. In purchasing custom-made items, Americans were implicitly acknowledging superior expert decorative skills of the Chinese that were either unavailable or too costly in the West. A case in point was the Pennsylvania Hospital bowl, which was originally commissioned to be done on English Staffordshire pottery, and was only made in China when difficulties arose between a London agent and the Staffordshire works.[29]

On the other hand, objects with purely Chinese motifs, in addition to being inexpensive and practical, had a particular aesthetic importance. Those objects with Chinese, rather than American, motifs gave the Westerner, in an era before the development of photography, his visual image of Cathay. Chinese people, landscapes, flora, fauna, and historical and mythological events were shown on porcelain, paper, fabric, wood, and glass. Legendary and historical events were depicted on Cantonese lacquer and silverware. An abundance of exotic blossoms and birds entered the American home on draperies. Wallpapers were veritable albums of Chinese life, illustrating methods of porcelain manufacture, or the cultivation of tea or silk. Those Americans who could not afford to hang Chinese drapes, or paper a room, might have been able to buy a Chinese painting of Canton, Macao, the Whampoa anchorage, the narrow defile on the Pearl River called the "Boca Tigris," or of the Fati Gardens which lay across the Pearl River from Canton. Album paintings on pith or "rice" paper were an even more widespread means of acquainting Americans with China. Inexpensive collections of these accurately drawn paintings, each dealing with a particular aspect of Chinese life, showed trades, occupations, ceremonies, processions, room interiors and furnishings, as well as flora, fauna, fishes, birds, and insects.

By virtue of its sheer quantity, pictures upon standard-issue porcelain were the commonest image of Cathay early Philadelphians got to see. Ceramics decorated in blue, orange, green, or sepia highlighted with gold brought a profusion of Chinese flowers, fruit, vegetables, insects, and birds into American households. These were painted with sufficient accuracy so that the guava, lotus, lichee, matrimony vine, luffa squash, rose, aster, peach, persimmon, and

Buddha hand citron, among other designs, could be readily iden-
tified. "Who could count," wrote the descendant of one China trade
captain, "the number of Americans who, while drinking morning
coffee or afternoon tea, gazed on the familiar motifs of islands,
pavilions, trees, and bridges, sometimes peopled, sometimes not. No
wares in the history of ceramics enjoyed such favor or were more
widely imitated. This beautiful, familiar, romantic-pattern touched
some chord of fantasy halfway around the world. It became the basic
symbol, the irreducible minimum; a breathless, motionless, timeless
image of China in the recesses of American consciousness."[30]

Thus, as a result of the China trade, Philadelphians were able to
"see" Cathay's natural history, its geographical features, field agriculture, pottery, metallurgy, architecture, script, mythology, and count-
less other cultural attributes. The image of China communicated
upon standard-issue artifacts, like the image conveyed in the mercantile correspondence which followed the first direct pioneering
voyage, was a positive one. Designs that were painstakingly drawn by
the Chinese themselves bore no characterization of biological or cultural inferiority; instead, the image came through of an agricultur-
ally and industrially productive, and artistically flourishing, culture.

While standard-issue Chinese goods filled both aesthetic and
utilitarian needs of Philadelphia consumers, another craft out of the
immensely rich Chinese imagination filled these needs to an even
more gradiose extent. The employment of Chinese architectural
motifs, and the respect for China which accompanied that utilization, will be discussed in the last chapter. Before proceeding to that
impressive usage, focus will shift from the imported Chinese designs
and goods themselves, back to the inflow of new wealth which these
products brought to the China traders. What these tycoons did with
their riches, and how their spending came to effect the region, has
yet to be discussed.

The Socialization of Wealth (I): The Reinvestment of China-Trade Profits

The profits earned by Philadelphia China traders were disbursed in
three principal ways. They were rechanneled into industries related
to the China trade, such as shipbuilding and supportive financial
institutions. They were ventured in unrelated enterprise, such as
land speculation, manufacturing, and new forms of transportation.
And they were bequeathed to public institutions.

It should be recalled that the primary derivative benefit of a

China trade, cited by Charles Thomson in his 1768 remarks and reiterated by other APS members, was to be the improvement of agriculture. They thought largely in terms of the introduction of new breeds and grafts. Such a process does occur in post-Revolutionary Philadelphia. The *Empress of China*, for example, shipped back Shanghai roosters, from which the "Bucks County chicken" was bred. Other voyages assembled collections of plants and other Oriental natural history specimens which were donated to Peale's Museum, the Wagner Free Institute of Science, and Pennsylvania Hospital, where they were studied. However, even greater social benefit derived to the region through the rechanneling of China trade profits into local industry.[31]

Philadelphia's shipbuilding industry expanded in response to the need for China clippers—a class of longer, faster, larger ships required for the China trade. Beginning in 1795, one Philadelphia shipyard built five ships for the China and East India trade, three of them over 400 tons, the other two over 300 tons. Girard, in the course of his career, owned eighteen ships, eight of which were locally built for the China trade. The nautical history of the blue-pennanted Girard fleet may be cited as an example of the far-reaching industrial and technological ramifications of the China trade, and of the ways in which one investor rechanneled his profits back into his business.

With the knowledge he gained from correspondence, plus his previous experience as a sea captain, Girard became a promoter of many of the new forms of transportation technology of his day. Although he declined opportunities to invest in telegraphic communications, steam navigation, and marine railways, Girard personally devised his own method of hauling his ships out of the water. He and his shipbuilders utilized a system of cables, attached to the capstans of his ships, to haul the vessels aground. Girard elongated one of his ships by cutting it in half and inserting a midsection of twenty or thirty feet.

In the construction of ships for his fleet, the spacecraft of their day, Girard utilized the most advanced models and materials. Finding that white oak did not wear well in warm climates, he ordered his ship *North America* built "solely with a live oak frame and knees," and with a hull sheathed in imported English copper.[32] The *Rousseau* was also made of live oak, and the *Voltaire* of a combination of live oak and cedar. It was reported that when the bottom of the *Rousseau* was replanked in 1879, her floor timbers were as firmly on her keel as when constructed. The nautical expert M. V. Brewington asserted that Girard's ships such as the *Montesquieu* or the *North*

America were probably the finest merchant sailing vessels ever constructed in the United States at any time.[32] Girard himself was so conscious of the technical superiority of at least the *Voltaire* that he insisted on paying a premium 1 or 2 percent below the common rate of insurance for that vessel.[33]

Thomas Cope (1768–1854), a major rival of Girard in the shipping business, also was a firm believer in innovation. After a propitious start in the China trade before the War of 1812, Cope had, by 1821, established the first regular transatlantic packet line, connecting Philadelphia with Liverpool.

In the broader aspects of their investments, China traders were closely associated with the founding and capitalization of national financial institutions that assisted their trade. Insurance companies provided the dual services of guaranteeing against losses and lending funds. Philadelphia China traders were closely affiliated, both in directorship and in volume of business, with INA, the Phoenix Insurance Company (Truxtun and John Latimer), the Insurance Company of Pennsylvania (Girard), the Atlantic Insurance Company (Ashabel Ralston), and the Franklin Insurance Company (Mordecai Lewis, Tobias Wagner, Thomas I. Wharton, and Charles N. and James A. Bancker). Cope appears to be the only Philadelphia merchant who permitted his cargoes to go uninsured. Since the China trade frequently involved full war-risk premiums, he felt that, with the savings on insurance, he could build more ships than he would lose.[34]

Girard is closely associated with the founding of the First Bank of the United States. He also loaned $4.5 million to the United States government in the War of 1812, subscribed $1.2 million toward his own bank in that same year, and $1.5 million toward the Second Bank of the United States in 1816. He let his maritime trade provide the capital for his banks and loans, not vice versa. Consequently, Girard took the unusual step of permitting some of his archrivals in the shipping business, including Cope, Robert Waln, Sr., and Samuel and Tobias Wagner to sit on the board of his bank, directing local disbursements, but unable to interfere with his maritime affairs.[35]

The scope of China traders' investments in diverse areas unrelated to the trade can only be suggested here. By 1830, Girard had purchased many blocks of Philadelphia real estate, large tracts of Lehigh County coal lands, and an estate in what is today Girardville, Schuylkill County. His extensive investments in internal transportation seem to have commenced in 1809, when he was the principal participant in the construction at Columbia, Pa., of the first bridge across the Susquehanna. In 1823, he loaned $230,000 to the

Schuylkill Navigation Company, a loan that was renewed two years later. In 1823, he was one of the incorporators of John Stevens' "Pennsylvania Railroad" from Philadelphia to Columbia. He also desired another railroad that would carry the produce of northern coal lands to Philadelphia. Consequently, in 1826, he subscribed $200,000 toward the building of a spur connecting Pottsville on the Schuylkill Navigation Canal with Sunbury on the Susquehanna, a line which is today's Reading Railroad.[36]

The portfolios of other Philadelphia China traders are dull by comparison with Girard's extensive interests, but do give further evidence of diversification. Thomas Fitzsimons had, at an early date, followed Morris' example and sent his own ship to Canton. By 1790, he had spread his interests into banking, government securities, and, in partnership with Morris, land speculation. Robert Waln, Sr., during the War of 1812, built a cotton factory on his property near Trenton, N.J., and invested heavily in the Phoenixville Iron Works. John Latimer invested the proceeds of an 1822–23 China voyage in the Phoenix Insurance Company and the Chesapeake and Delaware Canal Company, to which venture Girard, Cope, Samuel Archer, and Joshua Gilpin also subscribed. In 1829, Latimer sent his brother Henry $20,000 from Canton to be invested in diversified stateside interests. Apparently, he had already begun to think in terms of leaving China and did not wish his capital reinvested in the China trade.[37]

One of the commercial effects of the reinvestment of China-trade profits was to cause Philadelphia's mercantile separateness from other American emporia to wane somewhat. In part, due to the efforts of China traders, transportation and communication between American cities improved. Merchants took the initiative in organizing banks, insurance companies, and trading corporations active outside of the immediate region. Nationally negotiable stocks and bonds were issued. Early in the China trade there is evidence of a voyage out of Philadelphia being funded by a New York insurance company, and of Philadelphia merchants helping to finance a voyage from New York to Canton and back.[38] Particularly in the early years of the China trade, however, the extent of a national economy should not be exaggerated. Many of the old forms continued, notably family enterprises. The Waln family alone included nineteen major investors and participants in Philadelphia's China trade, out of about seventy-five individuals.[39] Other Philadelphia clans prominent in the China trade included Archer, Blight, Donnaldson, Hallowell, Hollingsworth, Lewis, Perit, Ralston, Smith, Sword, Thomson, Tiers, Tolland, Wagner, Wetherill, and Wharton. These ties played a major role in the line of succession within firms, in the composition of Boards of Directors, and in the selection of stateside or foreign factors. A further illustration of the continued inbred nature of the city's mercantile community was the composition of the Board of Directors of the Insurance Company of North America, the city's preeminent underwriter, and occasional financier, of long-range voyages. From the time of the company's founding in 1792, up through 1846, twenty-four of the approximately seventy-five substantial participants in Philadelphia's China trade (shippers, investors, consignees) sat on the Board of this institution, many for lengthy stretches, one (John C. Smith) as president of the organization for fourteen years.[40]

The Socialization of Wealth (II): Largesse

A final way in which merchants disbursed their profits was through public beneficence, an activity of equal if not greater social utility to the region than the invested dollars. Many Philadelphia China traders seem to have fulfilled their ethical and moral aspirations through largesse. Dunn made a $20,000 gift to Haverford College in 1840 when that Friends' school was experiencing financial difficulties. William Wagner, Girard's apprentice and later competitor in the China trade, left a $350,000 endowment for the natural history museum and lecture series that bears his name. While the records of Pennsylvania Hospital and the Friends' Asylum (now Friends' Hospital) are replete with the gifts of China traders over the years, the single biggest public act of beneficence in early post-Revolutionary Philadelphia was Girard's $6,000,000 endowment of a nonsectarian school for orphans. This was the major and best-known portion of Girard's 1831 will. But nearly an equal amount of money went to other needed civic improvements, such as the paving and lighting of Philadelphia streets and the improvement of canal navigation in Pennsylvania. Girard's will is the first American document outlining the type of large-scale public beneficence that would be commoner later in the century, with such philanthropists as Andrew Carnegie.[41]

It should be noted that wealthy China traders from many other American cities also rose to prominence as highly innovative practitioners of philanthropy and social reform. Robert Bennet Forbes of Boston helped establish coastal lifesaving units and homes for aged sailors, and was captain of the *Jamestown*, which carried food to Ireland during the potato famine. Captain Frederick W. Macondray, who traded in China from 1832 to 1838, served as first mate aboard the *Jamestown* and was also instrumental in helping San Francisco quell the problem of bandit gangs in 1851. Abbot Abiel Low, a Russell & Co. partner for four years, later became commissioner of charities for Kings County, New York, and submitted a report, which was far in advance of its time, dealing with the effect of population increase and unsanitary conditions on the spread of poverty. John C. Green, also of Russell & Co., made substantial gifts to Princeton University, Princeton Theological Seminary, and many New York City charities.[42]

As these merchants won their fortunes, the China trade, in the Quaker City, wrought multifarious changes by early in the nineteenth century. On a much greater scale than in the Colonial period, the aesthetic and utilitarian productions of China had been imported. Profits made in the trade went into local industries both connected with and unrelated to Asiatic commerce, resulting in improved transportation, communication, and general business. As in other early American cities, the China traders of Philadelphia had become innovative practitioners of philanthropy and social reform.

In 1789, with Philadelphia's China trade out of its infancy, United States Representative Thomas Fitzsimons of Pennsylvania rose before the House and summarized the trade's history to that point. "The merchants of this country have been under the necessity of exploring channels to which they were heretofore unaccustomed," Fitzsimons advised. "At length they have succeeded in discovering one that bids fair to increase our national importance and prosperity, while at the same time it is lucrative to the persons engaged in its prosecution . . . the trade to China and the East Indies."[43] Fitzsimons echoed the optimism that had been voiced by Philadelphia China-trade pioneers from Franklin, Thomson, and Swain, through the Pembertons, to Ledyard, Morris, Shaw, Swift, Randall, and Girard. Although the trade's early years had ended, the adventure was far from over. As the eighteenth century drew to a close, economic problems began to emerge within the China trade that would require as much resourcefulness toward their resolution as had the development of the commerce in the first place.

Turkish opium plant

4 Philadelphians and the China Opium Trade: Commercial, Diplomatic, and Attitudinal Consequences

I am very much in favor of investing heavily in opium. While the War lasts, opium will support a good price in China.

—Stephen Girard[1]

Economic Preconditions of the Opium Trade

A persistent problem that plagued China traders, as they went about acquiring goods for the home market, was the vexing question of what cargo could be profitably brought to Canton. Several basic criteria had to be met. It had to be a commodity the Chinese wanted, which narrowed the field considerably. Any product picked up further than 1,000 miles away from Canton had to be highly valuable relative to its weight and bulk, or most of the sale price would go to offset freight costs. Ideally, it ought to be a product of a continuously expanding demand and constantly high price in Canton. In an era before modern means of transportation and communication, it was difficult to predict when one's competitors would arrive in Canton with precisely the same cargo, giving the cohong the opportunity to buy at rock-bottom price in a glutted market. Lastly, in the case of Philadelphia merchants with extensive trade to Northern European, Iberian, and Mediterranean ports, it ought to be a commodity whose trade could be readily integrated with American trade to Europe. It was universally realized in the Philadelphia mercantile community that profit was best generated through a rapid turnover of cargo, rather than the shipment of static cargoes like ginseng over extended routes. Ginseng, furthermore, was particularly prone to gluts in the Canton market as China neared its annual consumption ceiling of about 2,000 piculs (or $100,000 worth). The drug was not popularly consumed and remained an imperial monopoly item for the duration of the old China trade.[2] The acquisition of specie was not as difficult for Philadelphians as it was for merchants of other cities because of the established wealth of some merchants and the unusual credit resources open to virtually all solvent businessmen. Because of specie's availability and invariably satisfactory purchasing power at Canton, it was the cargo which Philadelphia merchants most frequently shipped. But merchants continuously sought rare hard goods that would be of even greater profitability than specie, and particularly the type which might generate an ever-increasing demand.

Some merchants used the variegated produce of the Pacific islands, much of it highly prized in Canton, as specie substitutes. Philadelphia merchants did make several efforts to strike up a regular avenue of trade in Pacific sea otter pelts, sealskins, and sandalwood. But the combination of natural disasters in those waters, the rapid disappearance of prized natural items, and the apparent impossibility of integrating such commerce with a lucrative and established European trade kept Philadelphia merchants out of the Pacific trade almost entirely. It became the province of merchants from Boston, Salem, and Stonington, Connecticut, who lacked the extensive European trade and financial resources that Philadelphians had enjoyed since Colonial times.[3]

Philadelphia merchants' dependence upon specie remained their own personal affair except in those few seasons when the balance of trade favored China. It was then that China traders were singled out in the public press as individuals who drained the new nation of much-needed wealth. "Since 1784 the trade has been constantly tending to the disadvantage of the Europeans (i.e., Westerners)," a writer advised in the *American Museum* in 1790. He added that imports into China from the West "hardly defray the first cost; and the exports have increased in a ratio beyond all conjecture." John Swanwick, a Congressional defender of China traders' tariff privileges, was taken to task in the pages of the *American Museum* in 1792 by Dr. Thomas Ruston. Ruston suggested that reconversion to the colonial trade system of buying China goods through European companies would be no greater drain on the American economy, and possibly less of a drain, than an independent China-trade establishment which had to be subsidized.[4] Faced with such criticism in the public press, Philadelphia China traders, in about 1800, redoubled their already earnest effort to find specie substitutes. One scheme which satisfied all of the economic criteria for a successful China trade was the importation of opium to China. However, such a trade, unlike legitimate Canton commerce, was in direct violation of Chinese law and brought Philadelphia merchants, for the first time in a hundred years of trading in Chinese commodities, face to face with novel problems of diplomacy and international law.

The British Opium Trade and the Initial American Reaction

In the 1780s and 1790s, Britain provided additional mercantile inspiration to Philadelphia China traders. The formula this time was the opium trade, which was designed to solve Philadelphia merchants' specie-substitute difficulties.

Philadelphia merchants were aware from contacts in Europe and Asia that as the British consolidated their hold on India in the 1770s they began to ship large quantities of Indian opium to China. The drug was not native to China, and for centuries the Chinese had imported it for medicinal purposes. It may have also been used to a limited extent as a narcotic, but the widespread habitual use of the drug does not seem to have taken hold in China until the mid-eighteenth century, after the introduction of smoking to China from the New World. Smoking opium was a more convenient and leisurely manner of ingesting the drug than eating it, and resulted in an increased popular demand for the preparation.

In 1800, the Chinese government banned the use and importation of opium because of the drug's lethal nature if habitually used, its consequent deleterious social effect, and because the favorable balance of trade which China had traditionally enjoyed with the West was rapidly deteriorating. Even though the trade had been declared illegal, Britain was reluctant to relinquish it, and devised an elaborate smuggling system that remained substantially unchanged from 1800 up through the 1830s. British ships brought opium from India and weighed anchor in the outer reaches of Canton estuary, beyond the normal range of patrol of the Chinese Customs Service. Chinese smugglers known as "shopmen" surreptitiously sailed out to the opium ships, paid in cash for the narcotic, and spirited it ashore. The British ships, loaded with Chinese silver, then sailed into Canton estuary and either invested all the specie in Chinese goods or saved a portion of it for future opium purchases in India.

Perhaps the smoothest aspect of the British system was that the British East India Company, although extensively involved in the sale and cultivation of opium in India, took no part in the actual transshipment of the drug to China, and reiterated this fact when Chinese officials contemplated closing down legitimate company trade in Canton. The actual freighting of Indian opium to China was subcontracted to private trade firms such as Jardine, Matheson & Co., Dent & Co., and occasionally after 1815, to American merchants like the Philadelphians Benjamin Wilcocks and John Latimer. The Company used the proceeds it derived indirectly from opium sales to the Chinese for the purchase of its own China goods. From 1800 to 1834, the Company purchased about three-quarters of all Chinese maritime exports, much of it with opium-trade silver.[5]

American merchants observed the smooth operation of the British opium system long before they themselves became involved in the commerce. Their opinions remained essentially unchanged during the period of their participation. Many of them came to see its "legitimacy" in the same way that the British did. Boston merchant Robert Bennet Forbes reflected that view when he wrote that "dealing opium was not looked upon by the British government, by the East India Company, or by the merchants as a smuggling transaction. It was viewed as a legitimate business as long as the drug was sold on the coast, outside the professed jurisdiction of China." For Forbes, and others, engaging in the opium trade entailed no moral crisis, and was a simple matter of following "the right example of England, the East India Company, the countries that cleared it for China, and the merchants to whom I had always been accustomed to look up to as the exponents of all that was honorable in trade."[6]

Despite Forbes' claims, the opium trade was not, in reality, a legitimate business comparable to the trades in tea, specie, ginseng, porcelain, and other commodities which Westerners and Chinese traditionally exchanged. Although the drug actually passed from Western hands to Chinese hands offshore, vital processes of the contraband trade did in fact occur in Canton, within the bounds of

Chinese jurisdiction. It was in Canton, and not aboard ships off-shore, where the operations center of the opium trade was located, where deals were finalized, and where English-language circulars regularly listed opium prices. Furthermore, it was in Canton where Western merchants habitually spent specie which they knew had been illegally obtained within China by native smugglers. The Chinese had the right, even in terms of Western law, to sequester, if not confiscate, such funds. Perhaps a more candid description of the traffic was offered by Philadelphia merchant John Latimer:

> You are aware that the trade in opium is illegal. The system is perfect. A dealer pays the money down and at the same time receives the order to go to the ship for it. We never see it at all. Foreign merchants reside here constantly who are known to have no other business than the opium and are never mentioned.[7]

An even blunter statement on the propriety of the opium trade, indicative of the lack of moral crisis in the minds of smugglers, was offered in 1829 by Philadelphian Benjamin Wilcocks. In that year, Wilcocks offered John Whitall the captaincy of the ship *New Jersey* on a China opium voyage. Whitall, although a bonafide captain who had previously been in charge of the *New Jersey* on a non-opium voyage, refused, on moral grounds, to accept Wilcocks' offer to partake in the drug business. Wilcocks was indignant at the moral stance taken by the captain, and wrote:

> I almost wished I had not heard his objections to going into our employ, which have lessened him in my opinion. I hope I have due and proper respect for the prejudices of my fellow man, but when a Captain stipulates for the particular articles which he will take on my ship, why let him go *you know where* for a cargo. I have done with him forever.[8]

Just as Wilcocks was not alone in his unabashed defense of the drug traffic, neither was Whitall in his moral opposition. There was a split in the Philadelphia mercantile community on this issue. It is clear, on the one hand, that a number of merchants saw nothing wrong with the commerce and, after an American trade was shown to be commercially feasible, actively participated in it. It is also true that about a dozen Philadelphia China merchants vigorously denounced the opium business. Those merchants who chose not to engage in transporting opium included Peter Dobell, William Wood, the Philadelphia employees of Nathan Dunn & Co. and Olyphant & Co., and of Wetmore & Co. after 1839.[9] The abstaining Philadelphians took the smugglers to task. They denounced the trade on legal and moral grounds. William Wood expressed the legal viewpoint when he criticized the business for being "flagitious" commerce. A book published by Nathan Dunn characterized the traffic as illicit. Dunn, it was explained, was never interested in the trade "to the amount of a dollar." Peter Dobell, arguing from a moral viewpoint, described the narcotic as pernicious. William Wood used that adjective, and also spoke of the ravages the poison committed.[10]

The question inevitably arises of how, in the face of such criticism, an otherwise upright individual like Latimer could have engaged in the opium trade. That merchant was, variously, the President of the Society of the Cincinnati, the individual who took charge of the illegitimate daughter of another trader who abandoned the child in China, and an outspoken advocate of mercantile ethics in other areas.[11] The answer to this question lies in the realization that apparently no one in nineteenth-century Philadelphia, other than the few Jeremiahs who have been noted, saw the opium trade as being inappropriate, even with its dreadful results. This was the era of De Quincey's *Opium Eater,* of Samuel Taylor Coleridge, and of other Westerners who practically lived on laudanum. To expect a man who is average for his age and even sensitive to some social problems to react to yet another one, and in a manner similar to the way we do today, is to forget a basic fact of historicity. Those who denounced the traffic were noble voices, but voices crying far ahead of their time in a wilderness of eighteenth- and nineteenth-century entrepreneurship. The opium trade was, in many respects, a typical business form of that era, sharing a common quality of brutality with other enterprises in which many of the traders were simultaneously engaged: privateering; the purchase and sale of indentured servants and redemptioners; and the extraction of "sweatshop" labor from early Pennsylvanians in the mines, mills, and aboard the merchant ships. Some considered the sale of laudanum to be less cruel than these other enterprises. When the Philadelphia social reformer Mathew Carey criticized the opium traders, he did so not for their activities abroad but rather for their abuse of workers on Pennsylvania canal projects, and within the cities.[12]

Reference may also be made, at this point, to the question of racism, and the degree to which it was or was not espoused by those who engaged in the opium trade. Did this insidious treatment imply a negative view of the Chinese race or culture? The shipment of even as diabolical a commodity as opium was, in the West, almost universally considered as part of free trade, as noted. Although the trade was exploitative, it did not connote racism any more than did exploitation in the above-named Pennsylvania enterprises, in which both victim and employer/persecutor were of the same Caucasian stock. Peter Dobell, who lived in Canton during the period of opium troubles, and opposed the trade, was explicit in blaming not only American entrepreneurs, but their native Chinese collaborators, for the difficulties that afflicted Westerners and Chinese alike in Canton. He avoided saying that the trade was conducted in racist fashion by Caucasians who made an assumption of Chinese backwardness or perversity.[13]

While "immoral" may not be an appropriate characterization of the opium trade, the "illegal" nature of the business, which many traders openly acknowledged, can not be downplayed in deference to the mores of the age. Opium merchants and refrainers differed significantly in their views on obeying some Chinese laws. The abstainer may be said to have taken a higher view of Chinese society than did the smuggler, in this single respect.

The refrainer's view was derived from principles of Western thought. Such nuances were not of concern to the Chinese, who took yet another view of opium smuggling. In the unique political philosophy of the Chinese, the ultimate objective of government was the setting in order of the whole known world, not just the Chinese state. The Emperor claimed to be the Son of Heaven and to rule supreme over all mankind. The Chinese did not even countenance an argument that acts which they considered illegitimate occurred beyond the range of their jurisdiction.[14]

Even before embarking on an opium trade of their own, American merchants were aware of the ongoing philosophical and legal conflict between Chinese officials and Westerners at Canton. Stephen Girard admitted that he had been informed that opium was "prohibited at Canton," yet he was also aware that "there is no difficulty in shipping" if the smuggler was prudent.[15] The Chinese had not yet made any forceful showing of their determination to halt the trade, which continued virtually unimpeded. The major obstacle American merchants faced was that they lacked a ready source for very large quantities of opium. Traditionally, Americans had exported small quantities of opium westward from India for medicinal uses in North America. But the British were understandably reluctant to let American traders ship large quantities eastward, except when their own shipping was incapacitated, as in 1815. By 1804, the Boston firm of J. & T. H. Perkins had advised its supercargoes to keep their eyes open for sources of large quantities of opium.[16]

Philadelphians Open an American Opium Trade

It was Philadelphia merchants who located an alternate source of opium in Smyrna, Turkey. Americans had been trading in this port under the auspices of the British Levant Company. The British, with a ready source of opium in India, had never taken a serious interest in shipping Smyrna opium around Africa or across the Levant to China. The Philadelphia merchants William Waln and R. H. Wilcocks were apparently the first to attempt this operation. Their major informant on the scheme's feasibility may have been William Stewart, a Philadelphian who had been United States Consul in Smyrna, and who returned to Philadelphia in late 1803 or early 1804. Waln and Wilcocks dispatched the brig *Pennsylvania* to Smyrna in 1804, with Stewart taking a small interest in the outbound cargo. The supercargoes of the vessel were the owners' kinsmen, Benjamin Wilcocks and his younger brother James. Benjamin later rose to prominence as the United States Consul at Canton, a job he held simultaneously with his position as one of that port's preeminent opium merchants. Under the supervision of the Wilcocks brothers, the *Pennsylvania* unloaded its cargo of tea, sugar, and spices, and took on fifty chests of Smyrna opium; forty-nine were consigned to the supercargo, and one to the brig's master as private speculation. Also taken aboard were 8200 Spanish dollars, no doubt because of the experimental nature of the other cargo.

In March 1805, the ship cleared from Smyrna for Batavia. The opium seems to have gotten as far as Batavia, but it is unclear whether the ship went on from there to Canton; the brothers seem to have been reluctant to take the contraband cargo all the way on the first experimental voyage. They themselves proceeded to Canton, where Benjamin remained. James returned to Philadelphia on the *Pennsylvania* and went back to Canton the following year as supercargo of the *Sylph*, bringing more Smyrna opium.

The first recorded arrival of an American opium ship in China occurred in June 1806, when the Baltimore brig *Eutaw* brought "twenty-six chests, fifty-three boxes" of opium to Canton. The following month the *Sylph* arrived with thirty-three cases. The ship also carried Spanish dollars, indicating that Philadelphia merchants were not confident enough in opium to send an entire shipload.

Waln and the Wilcocks had demonstrated the feasibility of two opium routes: Smyrna-Batavia and Smyrna-Canton. After 1815, they demonstrated the feasibility of limited opium shipment from India as well. Other Philadelphia firms were quick to follow in their footsteps. Willing & Francis, successor firm to Willing & Morris, may have shipped opium to China as early as 1805 aboard their ship *Bingham*. Girard and his employees and later competitors, the Wagners and Blights, took an early interest in the pioneer voyages. In January 1806, Girard wrote his supercargoes: "I am very much in favor of investing heavily in opium. While the War lasts, opium will support a good price in China."[17] Between 1804 and 1807, of the twelve United States ships which took on opium at Smyrna, seven came from Philadelphia, three from Baltimore, and two from Boston. American merchants purchased as much of the Smyrna crop as they could and hungered for more. As a result of the initiation of an American opium trade, Philadelphia merchants became less reliant on the British Levant Company in Smyrna and established agencies of their own in that port. In 1811, David Offley, of the Philadelphia shipping firm of Woodmas and Offley, settled permanently in Smyrna and established the first American commercial house in the Levant. All but twenty-four of the seventy-eight United States vessels that traded at Smyrna between 1811 and 1820 were consigned to Woodmas and Offley. The remainder were consigned to such Smyrna merchants as Dutilh & Co., who sent one of their kinsmen, Edward Dutilh, to Philadelphia in 1819 to facilitate stateside aspects of the commerce.[18]

Between 1805 and 1807, Americans annually sold in Canton between 100 and 200 chests of Smyrna opium, worth between $100,000 and $200,000. Approximately one-third to one-half of this total was shipped by Philadelphia firms. In the years after 1815, American shipments of Smyrna opium to China quadrupled over previous levels. Despite this dramatic upsurge, for the duration of the American Smyrna opium trade Britain annually shipped to China approximately twenty times as much Indian opium as the Americans were ever able to secure in Turkey.[19]

Despite the small scale of opium shipments, the drug did fulfill Philadelphia merchants' need for a reliable China-trade commodity. It was perhaps because of opium's unique qualities that merchants were reluctant to give it up even in the face of official Chinese opposition. In addition to being highly valued by the Chinese, opium had the unusual property of generating an ever-increasing demand for itself, at a consistently high price. It was very expensive relative to its bulk, and in this respect more valuable than specie. Perhaps most important for Philadelphia merchants, opium was a commodity whose shipment could be readily integrated with extant transatlantic commerce.

Philadelphians' Social and Business Relationships at Canton, 1784–1846

Opium smuggling generated increasing tension between Chinese officials and Americans in China. Amid this stress, Philadelphians resided with other Westerners in refined elegance in the foreign enclaves of Canton and Macao. The Westerners created a social life for themselves which eased the workaday tensions of the China trade. John Latimer wrote that "the old fashioned manners have been preserved in Canton and on arrival here, most men are admitted to better society than they have been accustomed to at home."[20] Frequent banquets and gatherings were held in the consulates, factories, and hotels. A Canton Regatta Club and Canton Billiards Room Association were organized. An English-language press thrived. The petty infighting between free traders like Latimer and the staunch defenders of British monopolistic rights gradually waned in the interest of foreign solidarity. A unified foreign Canton General Chamber of Commerce was organized in 1836. However, as early as 1830, at a New Year's celebration in the British factory in Canton, Latimer arose before a hundred guests and toasted "the progress and prosperity of the American government," a proposition that might well have elicited a violent response from a largely British audience in Canton not too many years earlier. Some seventy persons joined in the wedding festivities for the British missionary doctor Thomas Colledge and the American Caroline Shillaber in Macao in 1833. Latimer imported a band of Italian singers for the event.[21]

For young men, the American community in Canton offered the opportunity for the realization of diverse enterprises and schemes. William Wood, son of the Philadelphia actor of the same name, came to Canton in the 1820s originally as a clerk for Russell and Co. By 1827, with the backing of the Matheson family, he had founded the *Canton Register,* inaugurating English-language journalism on the China coast. He also may have been the individual who introduced photography to China, as he did later in the Philippines. In his spare time, he assembled the natural history collection that formed the nucleus of Philadelphia's "Chinese Museum," which will be discussed further on.[22]

At least three Philadelphia physicians—James Bradford, Elisha Kent Kane, and the missionary doctor Andrew Happer—took up practice in Canton, catering to both foreigners and Chinese. In 1844, Kane joined the missionary doctor Peter Parker in performing a surgical feat of record-breaking magnitude—the removal of an

8¾-pound tumor from the face of a Chinese beggar.[23] In what was perhaps a typical summation by a young man of his experience in China, Kane wrote:

> China had been my first field of action and responsibility. It was here that, casting off the dependence of a child, I assumed the duties of a man. I felt myself improving in my profession and advancing in experience. My debts had been paid, my position established.[24]

While relations between Americans and Chinese officials remained in a state of immobility if not deterioration because of the opium trade, there were established mechanisms through which some other types of disputes involving Americans at Canton were normally handled. These other quarrels, like the controversies over opium, fell into the broad category of problems of international and commercial law. There were disputes within the foreign community of Canton involving the recovery of debts. There were broader disagreements which impinged upon but were not particular to the Canton trade, such as those over European violations of American neutral rights. There were questions concerning retrieval of debts between American merchants and their native Chinese business colleagues. In the adjudication of these quarrels, the confrontation and overt hostility which characterized American relations with Chinese officials only occurred when established mediation procedures broke down.

Disputes between American and European merchants in Canton were frequently adjudicated in American or European courts—a procedure Girard resorted to twice in efforts to bring justice to two of his Canton supercargoes whom he accused of embezzling funds.[25] Disputes between Americans and European states were frequently settled through conventions of admiralty law and international law that had been utilized by Westerners for centuries. Girard was able to ransom his ship *Montesquieu,* with a China cargo aboard, after that vessel had been seized at sea by the British. A substantial upsurge in both British and French harassment of American shipping after 1793 rendered such conventions increasingly impotent as mechanisms of conflict adjudication. In 1800, the USF *Essex* was dispatched as far as Batavia to escort a group of American China-trade vessels. The failure of diplomacy and international legal mechanisms to stem the tide of European depredation of American neutral shipping culminated in war between Britain and the United States in 1812. In that conflict the first American naval station in the Pacific was established on the island of Nukuhiva, from which base the *Essex* again swept out to protect American China-trade vessels.[26]

Within a general atmosphere of trust, there were inevitably financial disagreements between Americans and Chinese. Both Chinese and American merchants went bankrupt owing each other large sums, notably Manhop's failure with debts of $33,600 due Nathan Dunn & Co. Bankruptcy was the one dilemma for which there was usually no recourse, and the malady seemed to plague American and Chinese merchants indiscriminately. There were few instances of Americans cheating Chinese or vice versa, and when these did occur, they were generally resolved without the types of major crises that were the norm in disputes between Westerners and Chinese officials. Americans frequently rendered aid to Chinese merchants in the retrieval of debts owed by other Americans. In 1813, the Chinese merchant Consequa enlisted the aid of Peter Dobell in reclaiming money he was owed. In 1822, Benjamin Wilcocks was the middleman in Keetshing's efforts to recover debts owed him by two Philadelphia merchants. Keetshing was successful in one case (Mr. Elfreth), unsuccessful in the other (Mr. Pleasants). In 1846, Shing-ho regained money he was owed by Samuel Wetmore through the intervention of Commodore James Biddle.[27] There appears to be no evidence of Philadelphia merchants blaming their Chinese colleagues, in racial terms, for their own errors or losses. One might reasonably expect that type of disparagement and backbiting if Philadelphians did in fact possess notions of Chinese racial inferiority.

The relationships of Philadelphia merchants with the Chinese government, on the other hand, were fraught with conflict due to their opening and prosecution of the opium trade. The diplomatic consequences of their opium trade remain to be discussed.

Philadelphia Merchants' Initial Conflict with the Chinese Government, 1800–21

Beginning in 1800, the existence of a contraband opium trade produced a nefarious power structure which came to affect the lives of most Chinese and Westerners in and around Canton. The structure had its origin in the essential need of the Western opium merchant for the complicity of Chinese officials appointed to prevent the trade, and for the cooperation of native Chinese in the distribution of the drug. Such collaboration was forthcoming, but at a substantial price. Latimer wrote that "all the Chinese traders fee the officers regularly for their connivance and it is smoked by all, from the highest mandarin down."[28] The term "officers" referred to the two highest imperial appointees in Canton: the Viceroy, who held su-

preme authority in most provincial matters, and the Hoppo, who
held independent jurisdiction in the areas of foreign trade and customs collection. In addition to the fees these officials legitimately
collected, they received bribes at the usual rate of $20 to $70 per
chest of opium landed in Canton. They were also paid in opium,
which they could either use or resell in competition with "legitimate"
smugglers. S. B. Rawle and others reported seeing large amounts of
the narcotic transferred directly from Western opium ships to boats
carrying the flags of the Viceroy, the Hoppo, and other high provincial officials. Captain James Goodrich of the ship *Galaxy* wrote in
1835 that the "Hoppo boat which lays along side to prevent smuggling is always ready & willing to be engaged in smuggling. They
require but little compensation for their services."[29]

The total eradication of the opium trade was not even contemplated by Canton officials, who were both habitual opium smokers
and receivers of enormous bribes for their complicity in the traffic.
Periodically, however, they were instructed from Peking to crack
down on the smuggling due to China's deteriorating balance of payments. Such occasions were opportunities for Canton officials to
profiteer even further while at the same time carrying out official
directives. The officers eliminated smugglers' boats that were im-
pinging on their own opium trade. Furthermore, they shut down the
cohong as a nominal means of pressuring Western opium traders,
and then wrung huge bribes from that same body as the price of
reopening. The process of "squeezing" the cohong, as it came to be
known, resulted in the rapid financial deterioration of that guild
after 1804. The excessive demands made on the cohong, particularly
during the 1817 *Wabash* incident and 1821 Terranova incident, produced numerous bankruptcies and withdrawals. The Viceroy had
difficulty recruiting other merchants to fill the vacancies. By 1839,
there were only two members of an organization which had had
several dozen in 1800.[30]

Because of periodic shutdowns of all legitimate trade, American
opium dealers and abstainers alike were kept under the thumb of
the most venal and corrupt Canton officials. A member of Olyphant
& Co. lamented that "our nation is involved in dishonor and perhaps
losses here for the sake of a few chests of opium, a mere trifle in
all."[31]

The existence of the opium traffic became particularly critical
for the Chinese economy after 1815. Before 1815, although British
and American opium traders were draining China of specie, Spanish
traders from Manila continued to pay for their Canton purchases in
New World cash. The influx of Spanish silver appears to have some-

what counteracted the outflow caused by the opium trade. However, beginning in 1815, Spanish silver shipments from Mexico and Latin America dwindled to naught because of turmoil in those possessions. Many Spanish China traders in Manila went bankrupt and subsequently joined English opium firms in India. The Spanish merchants added their long-term business experience in Southeast Asia to the comparatively recent expertise of the English. China's economy suffered on both these accounts.[32]

Increased Chinese opposition to the opium trade materialized early in 1815. In May of that year, Consul Wilcocks dissuaded a Chinese magistrate from searching his opium schooner *Lydia* through bluff and the timely misuse of his consular seal.[33] Five months later an imperial crackdown netted a gang of smugglers in the act of unloading opium from a Bengal ship. In the general search that followed, the supercargo of Girard's *Voltaire* had difficulty disposing of that vessel's opium. He wrote of "being under the necessity of sending it away by very small quantities for fear of detection."[34] In May 1817, at Consul Wilcocks' request, the Chinese government apprehended and executed pirates who had pillaged the Baltimore opium ship *Wabash*. When the Viceroy discovered that the ship carried opium, despite Wilcocks' care not to mention it, the official utilized the occasion for another all-out crackdown. The Hong merchants, pressured by the Viceroy, announced that they would thereafter refuse to secure ships whose masters had not signed bonds stipulating noninvolvement with the opium trade. Although this particular pledge was later relaxed, the cohong did issue the first formal notification specifically to Americans on the subject of opium. This memorandum, addressed to Wilcocks, exhorted the Americans that

> foreign opium is not allowed to come to Canton; if it is presumptuously brought, the moment it is discovered, it will immediately involve the security merchants; and the cause of the said vessel bringing the dirt for smoking to Canton will also assuredly be examined into; and a prosecution begun which will impede her departure.[35]

Neither this admonition nor the prior Chinese displays of determination to halt the trade resulted in any perceptible decrease in the traffic. In 1816–17, the season of the *Wabash* incident, foreigners unloaded 3,600 chests of opium in China worth $4.1 million; in 1817–18, 4,128 chests worth $4.2 million; in 1818–19, 5,387 chests worth $4.7 million; in 1821–22, 5,011 chests worth $8.6 million. The American share in the 1818–19 season was $434,000, only 10 percent of the seasonal total, but a clear indication of American non-compliance with the cohong's directive of two years earlier.[36]

In the fall of 1821, the most serious Chinese crackdown to date occurred in what has come to be known as the Terranova incident, named after the hapless Italian sailor who inadvertently precipitated the event. Because of the large number of American ships in Canton in the 1821–22 season, numerous eyewitness accounts of the incident have survived, from which it is possible to get a fairly clear picture of the event.[37] Francis Terranova, a sailor aboard the Baltimore opium ship *Emily,* was engaged in buying fish from a Chinese couple in a dinghy that had pulled alongside his ship. Suddenly, the woman fell overboard and drowned. The husband accused Terranova of having pushed the woman overboard, and demanded redress from the Canton authorities, who recognized the incident as another opportunity to crack down on the opium trade. The Canton authorities demanded that Terranova be surrendered to them for punishment. When his captain refused, the cohong was immediately shut down and foreign trade embargoed at Canton.

The members of the cohong, mercilessly "squeezed" from above, finally prevailed on the *Emily*'s captain to surrender Terranova, with the assurance that the sailor would be given a fair trial. The captain acquiesced. But, instead of a fair trial, Terranova was summarily strangled, without even the chance to present evidence on his own behalf. The Viceroy, after being heavily bribed, permitted trade to resume, after informing the Americans by edict:

> The ship came for no other purpose than to sell opium. Rightly did heaven send down punishment and cause Francis Terranova to commit a crime for which he was strangled.[38]

The hypocrisy of the edict, the outrageous nature of the "trial," the major disruption of trade, and the realization by traders that the volatile situation would endure as long as American contraband trade existed, caused great concern to American merchants. A Girard supercargo wrote from Canton:

> What further trouble the hong merchants may have I know not, but I really fear it will cause all the ships some attention. I am in hopes to get away for all has been here for the last six weeks in a very unsettled state.[39]

A European correspondent of Girard, on learning of the Terranova incident, wrote him warily:

> Till now reports of the European trade in China about to experience much difficulty has had no influence on this arti-

cle [tea] here, but if they be confirmed an augmentation [of difficulty] may be expected.[40]

The prospect of continued difficulty in prosecuting the opium trade and in resolving disputes with Canton authorities seem to have been the critical factors which induced Girard and John Jacob Astor, two of the most successful American China traders, to significantly scale down their China operations after the Terranova incident. Astor withdrew from the China trade entirely. Girard sent two more voyages to Canton, his final one in 1824. The combination of venality of officials and unpredictability of conditions at Canton had made trade even in as lucrative a commodity as opium a poor business risk for these merchants. As these traders withdrew, a more vigorous kind of American entrepreneur remained in Canton to conduct business in an ever more volatile atmosphere.[41]

Philadelphia Merchants' Final Conflict with the Chinese Government, 1821–46

The increased Chinese militancy toward the American opium trade, beginning in 1815 and culminating in the Terranova incident of 1821, resulted in a major reshuffling of attitudes within the American community in Canton after 1821. Up to the Terranova incident, the basic attitude had been to try and live with the exactions of the Chinese. Thomas Randall, of the *Empress of China,* was perhaps the first American to enunciate this view in 1791:

> The idea of a representation, concerning the frauds and impositions of the Chinese to the Emperor, would deserve attention were there not the danger of making things worse.[42]

As late as 1819, American merchants, not wishing to antagonize the Chinese, had rejected the proffered protection of one of their country's naval units when it touched at Canton. Latimer had expressed the view that "to contend with the Chinese would be madness. If they refuse to listen to our terms we have no recourse."[43]

Part and parcel of the American policy of passivity was a willingness to accept those rights and privileges that Britain secured from the Chinese and that were extended to other Westerners as a matter of course. "We will not oppose you," Latimer informed his British colleagues in 1829. "Gain all you can, we are sure to come in for the benefits."[44] The most notable success achieved by this policy occurred in 1842, when the hard-won rights and privileges which China granted to Britain in the Nanking Treaty were extended to the United States some two years before the conclusion of the first Sino-American treaty. The policy of passivity enabled Americans to present themselves to the Chinese as friends and allies, in ready contrast to the belligerent British, and yet to wind up with essentially the same gains as Britain.[45]

In addition to American willingness to accept privileges secured by the British, the American traders in Canton engaged in a delicately orchestrated diplomacy of their own. The supreme caveat in the diplomacy was that under no circumstances should the risk be run of having the Canton market closed to American shipping. All other projects and propositions might be entertained. There was continuous Congressional lobbying by China traders for the upgrading of the United States Canton consulate into more than a ceremonial and unsalaried post. Repeated requests were made for the stationing of an American physician in Canton, attached to the consulate. This demand was fulfilled in 1827 when Dr. James Bradford of Philadelphia took up residence in Latimer's house in Canton and opened a practice. As early as 1821, prior to the Terranova incident, Robert Waln, Jr., advocated in a series of articles in Philadelphia's *National Gazette* that an American embassy be sent to China and a commercial treaty negotiated.[46]

All of these suggestions, insofar as they required Chinese compliance in their implementation, overlooked the fact that the imperial Chinese government would be averse to enter into negotiations with Western powers so long as a contraband opium trade continued, as it did increasingly in the years after the Terranova incident. Latimer took over the opium trade of Benjamin Wilcocks when that entrepreneur returned to the United States in 1827. He expanded both the India and Turkey branches of the American trade, and stationed an opium-receiving ship in the outer reaches of Canton harbor. That vessel, the *Thomas Scattergood,* cleared some $30,000 for Latimer in the course of its operation. During the six seasons 1822–23 through 1827–28, foreign sales of opium in China annually averaged 8,043 chests, worth $8.7 million. The average of the next six seasons rose to 17,756 chests, worth $13.4 million. In the single season of 1837–38, foreign opium sales in China reached a record high of 28,307 chests worth $19.8 million, or more than double the annual average of the previous ten seasons.[47]

The increase in contraband traffic, far from inducing the imperial government to grant concessions to Westerners, instead elicited increasingly militant Chinese efforts to halt the traffic. These efforts, in turn, evoked a heightened militancy among the determined traders who had survived the Terranova incident. American traders reconsidered their previous aversion to American naval involvement in China. The USF *Congress* had received a cool if not unfriendly reception from Americans and Chinese alike when it touched at Canton several times in 1819. When the USF *Vincennes* anchored at Whampoa in 1830, Latimer, W. H. Low, and other American merchants informed the captain that "delays and impositions peculiar to our flag" could be easily corrected by frequent visits to Canton of American men-of-war. In a lengthy memorial to the captain of the *Vincennes,* the American traders advised:

> Our national character would be elevated in the estimation of the whole Chinese Empire and the neighboring governments, and especial care would be observed by all not to encroach on our rights, knowing that the power to protect the very valuable commerce of our country was at hand to appeal to, and that the appeal would not be made in vain.
>
> The fact of your visit, brief as it is, will be known throughout China and the whole Indian Archipelago. Should it be followed by those of other armed vessels observing the same deference towards the customs of China, and conciliatory disposition as exhibited by yourself, they will in our opinion increase the respect for our flag, enable us at all times to resist impositions with effect, and have a moral influence on all the inhabitants of the various coasts and islands in the route of our merchant ships.[48]

American merchants were in effect requesting an increased display of what the British called "military presence." In the years subsequent to the merchants' petition, American men-of-war did touch at Canton several times. But far from having the "moral effect" on the Chinese government which the traders desired, the situation in Canton escalated into open warfare.

In 1838, the Chinese Emperor abandoned efforts to halt the opium trade through the medium of Canton civil servants. He appointed Lin Tse-hsu, Viceroy of Hu-kuang, as a special imperial commissioner authorized to stop the opium trade in Canton province. Lin arrived in Canton on March 9, 1839. On March 22, he employed the technique of embargoing trade and sequestering foreigners, but this time the objective was the confiscation of all opium in the region. Lin further insisted that all foreign traders post bond consenting to the forfeiture of any of their ships on which opium might be found. The situation remained in deadlock on April 28 when the USF *Columbia* coincidentally sailed into Canton on one of its periodic visits. Some hostages in the confined foreign community considered the ship's arrival providential, and were bitterly disappointed when the ship's commodore declined to attempt to rescue them, on the grounds that the hostages were too few, and the enclave too well surrounded. The British and Americans subsequently acceded to Lin's demand for the confiscation of all opium in Canton, worth some $12,000,000, as the price of lifting the siege. The British Superintendent of Trade in China, Captain Charles Elliot, refused, however, to sign the bond. He ordered all British merchants out of the city of Canton and requested British military assistance to redress what he saw as a flagrant violation of free trade. A British fleet arrived in 1840, initiating the Opium War. The Americans, on the other hand, signed a modified version of the opium bond, and by July 1839 were actively reengaged in Canton commerce, carrying their own legitimate trade plus that of Britain, which more than compensated for the temporary loss of the opium trade.[49]

The American decision to acquiesce was based on the twin assumptions of the futility of direct and forceful confrontation with Chinese government officials, and the profitability of letting Britain do precisely that, while Americans posed as friends and allies. S. B. Rawle, James Ryan, and others wrote that the voluntary American pledge to abstain from the opium trade was motivated by their belief in the "sincerity of the Government in their efforts to destroy the trade." When the British expeditionary force arrived in China in 1840, William Waln, unsure of the outcome of a Sino-Western military confrontation, wrote that "the Chinese are making every effort to resist and I do not believe the land force (5,000) sent by England can do anything towards attacking Pekin. That is the only way they can bring the Emperor to terms."[50] Rawle, Ryan, and others petitioned their government in 1839 to avoid military confrontation with the Chinese. But they stressed the value of military presence and diplomatic gestures as means of protecting American noncombatants in the Anglo-British conflict and at the same time obtaining without bloodshed certain key concessions: a commercial treaty; a fixed tariff; freedom to trade at ports other than Canton; compensation for losses incurred during Chinese trade stoppages (as in 1839); diplomatic relations at Peking; and a demand just short of extraterritoriality (that no Chinese punishment upon an American exceed a comparable chastisement in American or English law).[51]

William Waln's estimation of the military aspects of the conflict proved to be incorrect. Britain's modern navy inflicted a crushing defeat on the Chinese, who readily acceded to all British demands, including repayment for the confiscated opium. Peking did not have to be occupied. A peace treaty was signed at Nanking in 1842, which opened five more ports to Britain, abolished the cohong, established a uniform tariff, and ceded Hong Kong to Britain.

In response to the urgent requests of American merchants at Canton, an American fleet under Commodore Lawrence Kearny arrived in Canton harbor in March 1842, where it remained without engaging in combat until May 19, 1843. Kearny was able to secure for American traders, through direct negotiation with the Canton Viceroy Ch'i-ying, many of the concessions suggested in the 1839 Rawle-Ryan petition and virtually all of the privileges granted Britain in the Nanking Treaty, except for the establishment of a colony. Kearny procured Chinese reparation payments for two violations of American neutral rights during the Opium War.

Most important, Kearny helped to lay the diplomatic groundwork for the first Sino-American treaty. He asked President Tyler that the rights and privileges he had secured be codified in a formal agreement. In response to Kearny's request and the lobbying efforts of American traders and missionaries, Caleb Cushing was sent to China in 1844, and incorporated many aspects of the existing Sino-American entente into the first Sino-American treaty, known as the Wanghsia Treaty. In addition to privileges granted in the Nanking Treaty, the Wanghsia document guaranteed Americans the right of extraterritoriality, eliminating many of the jurisdictional questions that had arisen as a result of opium smuggling.

In spite of the desire of American merchants that the negotiations with the Chinese be peaceful, there was one military encounter between Americans and Chinese. In July 1844, while deliberations were in progress, a Canton mob surrounded the American compound and marines were landed from Cushing's ship to break the siege. The skirmish that ensued was the first instance of the use of the American armed forces on the Asiatic mainland, although in this case the action appears to have been clearly defensive, and intended to prevent even greater carnage than what actually did occur.

In December 1845, Commodore James Biddle brought to China the ratified version of the Wanghsia Treaty and established the first United States embassy in China. The treaty went into effect in April 1846.[52]

The End of Philadelphia's Old China Trade

While the First Treaty Settlement elicited hopes and expectations for new and expanded Sino-American relations, many of the attributes of the old China trade quickly became extinct. The highly regulated trade through the Canton cohong was replaced by open markets in five new Chinese ports, as well as in the British Crown Colony of Hong Kong, which had the finest natural harbor facilities on the China coast. In 1848, regular transpacific steamer service was inaugurated between Hong Kong, the Hawaiian Islands, and San Francisco. The completion of the first trans-American railroads shortly thereafter eliminated the need of sailing around the Capes to China. Philadelphia and other East Coast cities could import China goods more cheaply overland from the West Coast than by a direct sea route from China.

An old China-trade firm wishing to remain in business after the First Treaty Settlement had to rapidly undergo at least two transitions. It had to expand its Chinese operation to at least Hong Kong and Shanghai, if not to all of the open ports. Most American China-trade firms were able to complete this first phase shortly after 1842. Augustine Heard and Co. was the last significant American firm to remain in Canton, and it shifted its headquarters to Hong Kong in 1853. Firms were also faced with the necessity of developing new facilities on the American West Coast. In the case of Philadelphia firms, branches or outlets also had to be established in New York, which by 1846 had become the emporium of the United States, the port which handled virtually all direct Asiatic maritime shipping to the East Coast.

Small entrepreneurs could not make all of these costly and extensive transitions. The weeding out of the weak from the strong, a process evident in the old China trade as far back as 1821, took on new impetus as a result of the First Treaty Settlement. Only two firms with strong Philadelphia connections were able to make the transition: Wetmore & Co. (which ultimately succumbed to bankruptcy in 1856) and the dynamic two-man firm of John D. Sword & Co. They competed in a new China trade dominated by a few shipping giants with fleets of vessels and worldwide buying and marketing apparatuses: Jardine, Sassoon, Olyphant, Heard, Russell, and its offspring, the Shanghai Steam Navigation Company.

After 1848, just as New York came to handle virtually all the direct China trade to the American East Coast, San Francisco rose to prominence as the major entrepôt for West Coast China commerce. That trade pattern remained essentially unchanged from 1848 until 1950, when the United States embargoed all maritime trade with the newly formed People's Republic of China. That embargo was modified as a result of Chinese-American negotiations in the 1970s. American ships once again began docking at the old treaty ports of the China coast, but originating from such new and diverse locations as Port Seatrain and Pascagoula, as well as Philadelphia and other established ports of the American East Coast.

Because of inconsistency in nineteenth-century foreign-trade statistics, it is difficult to calculate precisely Philadelphia's share in overall eighteenth- and nineteenth-century American commerce with the Orient. It does appear, as at least one scholar has observed, that between 1783 and 1846 Philadelphia may have controlled as much as one-third of United States trade with China, and one-ninth of China's total maritime commerce with the West.[53] This determination is based on the fact that from 1804 through 1811 (the years for which the most detailed statistics are available), Philadelphia ships unloaded 38 percent of the dollar value of United States imports to China, or $10 million out of the $25.8 million. In terms of gross tonnage, Philadelphia shipping was 32 percent of total American tonnage in the China trade in the years 1804–11 (20,406 tons out of 62,851 tons). That percentage was a considerable drop from the year 1787, when Philadelphia shipping constituted over 50 percent of United States tonnage in Canton, but was an average maintained fairly consistently from about 1800 to the mid-1830s, when the percentage again began to decline. In terms of entries to the Port of Canton, Philadelphia ships also made up approximately 30 percent of the American total. In terms of composition of cargo, specie constituted 38 percent of the overall dollar value of American imports to China, yet made up 45 percent of Philadelphia imports. Philadelphia merchants' opening and development of the opium trade is all the more understandable in this context.[54]

The structure of Philadelphia enterprise at Canton, as has been suggested, closely paralleled the inbred nature of commerce in the home port. The Canton trade of Benjamin Wilcocks, John Latimer, James Bancker, and John Dorsey Sword was overwhelmingly Philadelphia-oriented, toward the merchants they and their families had been dealing with for generations. These men included Girard, the Walns, the Archers, the Thomsons, Manuel Eyre, Charles Massey, George Jones, and Richard Oakford. The growth of Wetmore & Co. into the second biggest mercantile firm on the China coast was facilitated by the successive mergers of the Canton business of the Philadelphians J. S. Wilcox, Benjamin Wilcocks, John Latimer, Joseph Archer, Jabez Jenkins, and Nathan Dunn.[55]

The China trade facilitated a worldwide circulation of wealth. Practically every known port and trade route of the eighteenth and nineteenth centuries was utilized by the China trade. Sometimes traders like Robert Morris or Ledyard individually attempted to discover new avenues for the China trade. Other times large numbers of

American China traders descended en masse on ports like Smyrna, where they established branches of their own firms to facilitate the China trade. Capital circulated continuously from East to West, West to East, creating industrial and social transformations as it moved. American China traders reinvested their wealth not only in stateside ventures but also in such Chinese enterprises as the Shanghai Steam Navigation Company—a joint venture with the heirs of Houqua. They also financed charitable projects in China on a scale comparable to stateside public endowments, for example, the Canton Hospital, established in 1835. Native Chinese merchants also ventured their capital in worldwide investments that included American railroads and the financing of the American opium trade to China.[56]

And what of the opium trade—the nominal reason for which the Opium War had been fought? American merchants did keep their pledge to abstain from the opium traffic during Sino-British hostilities, and augmented their fortunes through the carriage of British trade. No sooner had hostilities ended than the illicit trade resumed in full force all along the China coast. Olyphant and Wetmore continued to abstain. But a weak and downtrodden Chinese government, beset with full-scale civil war by midcentury, was unable to put up any resistance at all to the traffic after 1839. In 1858, the Chinese legalized and for the first time imposed a tariff on the importation of opium, hoping to at least gain some revenue from a traffic which had thrived underground for fifty-eight years. A British visitor to China in that year reported that the sale of opium was "as open and as unrestrained in all the cities of China as the sale of hot cross buns on Good Friday in the streets of London."[57] William B. Reed, the American Minister to China, reported in that same year that "at every port, I found Americans dealing in opium freely and unreservedly, and at least one American built, but British owned steamer, with the American flag, plying regularly up and down the coast as a quick carrier of the poison." Between 1875 and 1885, opium was China's single largest import in dollar value. The end of the foreign opium trade to China came early in the twentieth century, when the Chinese government bowed to the interest of native Chinese opium growers and imposed such high import duties on the drug that the Indian, British, and American traders were forced from the trade entirely.[58]

In concluding this chapter on the opium trade, and prior to an overall survey of Philadelphia attitudes toward the Chinese, it might be well to summarize the attitudes which Philadelphia smugglers took toward the Chinese race and culture, and toward the propriety of the trade.

Although Philadelphia opium traders did exploit the Chinese people by opening and prosecuting a trade in an addictive poison, this treatment of the Chinese was considered by American traders as part of free trade, and did not imply that merchants had assumed a negative view of the Chinese race or culture.

The legitimate merchant and smuggler substantially differed in attitude over the issue of respect for some Chinese laws. The opium merchant violated these far more than his legitimate competitor. Yet even in the area of respect for the law, it is clear that many militant abstainers flouted other Chinese laws when such behavior suited their commercial purposes, such as in requesting American military intervention in China.

A strong similarity of belief between abstainer and smuggler appears when one considers aspects of China other than its government. A distinct example of this convergence of view was the great respect both types of trader accorded to the Chinese merchant class. Because of the central role of native Chinese businessmen in East-West interaction, they are singled out, by traders and abstainers alike, as a group of Chinese especially deserving of esteem and trust. Such commentary dates from the first U.S.-China voyage of the *Empress of China* in 1784. Robert Morris and others with an interest in that ship's legitimate cargo were informed by the supercargo that Chinese merchants were "respectable men, exact accountants, punctual to their engagements, and value themselves much upon maintaining a fair character."[59] Similar high praise for the Chinese recurred in the mercantile correspondence of Philadelphians who entered the opium trade after 1800. Stephen Girard considered Houqua both a "correct and intelligent merchant" and "my respectable friend." Esching was "of good repute, very polite, and a good judge of teas." These Chinese merchants bestowed Girard with such gifts as life-size paintings of themselves and lacquered tea chests. Girard prominently displayed these gifts in his Philadelphia counting house and also instructed that they be permanently exhibited in Founder's Hall, Girard College, under the terms of his will. Benjamin Wilcocks commissioned a personal portrait of his friend Houqua. Jacob Waln wrote Houqua's nephew Lin Yan-ken that any package bearing Lin's seal was sufficient assurance of quality. He also hoped for personal visits between the Lin and Waln families, a wish which was subsequently realized in the visits of the heirs of these two merchants to each other's nations. One of Lin's descendants came to America in 1872 as a member of the first official group of Chinese students in the United States.[60]

It should be noted that, in the writings of both opium and non-opium traders from United States cities other than Philadelphia, there was also an expression of high opinion for Chinese merchants. William Hunter wrote that "as a body of merchants, we found them honorable and reliable in all their dealings, faithful to their contracts, and large-minded." He singled out Houqua as having "boundless" generosity.[61] John Murray Forbes' grandson, looking back on the long history of relations between his and Houqua's families, praised the Cantonese businessman as having been "scrupulously honest" in his financial and commercial transactions. So impressive was Houqua's trustworthiness that "his name has come down for generations as the last word in probity, sagacity, and generosity. His painted portrait hung on the walls of many American houses, highly prized as the symbol of all that is praiseworthy in public and private relations."[62] Other traders published tales of how they were befriended by Chinese businessmen, and a great clipper ship was named for Houqua. When that Hong merchant died, Benjamin Low eulogized his Chinese colleague as being "in every inch the mannered gentleman" and of an "inviolate word," comments which were typical of praise for Chinese traders from Philadelphians and others.[63]

Thus far, the views of individuals who were primarily businessmen in post-Revolutionary America have been emphasized. What remains to be examined for the post-Revolutionary period are the attitudes of individuals who may be considered primarily men of arts and letters.

Nathan Dunn's "Chinese Cottage,"
Mount Holly, New Jersey, 1832

5 Sinophiles and Sinophobes in Post-Revolutionary Philadelphia: The Question of Attitude

One topic which has not been dealt with heretofore in this study is the overall ways, in the post-Revolutionary period, in which Philadelphia intellectuals came to view the Chinese race and culture. We have seen respect in the Colonial period. We have noted the positive views of the traders in the early post-Revolutionary period. In that era commentators voiced the twin assumptions that the China trade was to be of unprecedented economic importance for the new nation; and, because of that great commercial value, the Chinese people as a whole should be held in esteem. We have seen the disrespect which Philadelphians showed for the Chinese government in the post-Revolutionary period. But the Chinese government was only one single aspect of China about which opinions were formulated.

In order to determine what the overall image of the Chinese people was among men of arts and letters in post-Revolutionary Philadelphia, two types of evidence will continue to be examined: material culture and literary commentary. This evidence can provide a useful test of the explanations historians have advanced concerning the degree to which racism permeated early Sino-American relations. According to the traditional view, until at least the outbreak of the Opium War in 1839, excellent business and personal relations existed between Americans and Chinese. Although friction did occur between Americans and the Chinese government, this conflict did not have racial overtones. An alternative explanation alleged a substantial incidence of racism and deprecation of the Chinese in biological terms. According to that theory, Americans held negative opinions of the Chinese as a whole, and these negative reactions were communicated to a broader public in published accounts.

Before proceeding to the body of evidence which indicates the existence of positive views and is supportive of the traditional consensus, the negative reactions which some Philadelphians unquestionably had toward the Chinese should be noted. These highly prejudiced views were taken of both the Chinese race and its cultural productions. The most outspoken Philadelphia exponent of this viewpoint was the merchant James Bancker, a Philadelphian resident in Canton. Bancker left abundant and vivid commentary concerning the "dirty and impudent" Cantonese. Among his most disgusting recollections of Canton were those occasions when he ventured forth from the refined elegance of the foreign enclave and was obliged to "jostle along with a crowd of dirty Chinamen, who sometimes accost you with the cry of Fanqui lo (foreign devil get out)."[1] Additional criticism of the Chinese people in terms that approached racism appeared anonymously in the Philadelphia magazine *Port Folio*. One of the magazine's editors, Charles Caldwell, Professor of Natural History at the University of Pennsylvania, was a key figure in the early evolution of the scientific racist theory of the "American School" of ethnology. Caldwell may have used the magazine as a medium through which he could attack the accepted monogenesis theory of the unity of mankind advanced by Rush and others in the eighteenth century, and offer in its place a theory of discontemporaneous, and inherently unequal, racial origins. An anonymous 1811 *Port Folio* article asserted that the Chinese and Tartars resembled each other in the "idiocy" of the two peoples. The Chinese examination system was "silly" and her Great Wall a "huge memorial· of folly." The "genius" of the Chinese people was manifest "only when impelled by necessity, their mental subjection begetting incapacity."[2] An 1819 article declared that the Chinese "never can become a great and independent people" because they were "constitutionally, a feeble race of men." The author, a Philadelphian who claimed a long residence in Canton, observed that the Chinese exhibit a most deplorable contrast to everything that is great, wise, noble, and honorable. They are literally a flock of sheep in comparison with Europeans and their army of millions would be as easily routed and slaughtered.[3]

Apart from these examples of anti-Chinese sentiment, there is a much larger body of evidence indicating that early Philadelphians admired the Chinese, and particularly their cultural productions. Reference has already been made to the fact that during the Colonial period and up to about 1810, when the racist pundits of the *Port Folio* became active in Philadelphia, other scholars produced research of an opposite vein. These studies not only downplayed the physiological and cultural differences which set Chinese and Americans apart. They also stressed the practical value of adapting to America many of the advanced cultural features of Chinese society. Commercial relations between the United States and China were the mechanism whereby this cultural interchange could take place.

From the early nineteenth century on, APS members and other Philadelphia intellectuals continued researches along the lines initiated in the Colonial period, researches which far outweighed the negative publicity given China and the Chinese by the few racists. There was an increase in the utilization of various types of Chinese technology in Philadelphia, particularly in the areas of agriculture, architecture, and landscaping. Museums and other public displays about the arts of China were assembled in Philadelphia. Published scholarship continued to convey a positive image of the Chinese and their culture.

The Utilization of Chinese Technology: Agriculture, Architecture, and Landscaping

It should be recalled that one of the primary derivative benefits of the China trade, noted by Charles Thomson in the Colonial period, was to be the improvement of American agriculture and industry. In the post-Revolutionary period, to an even greater extent than in the Colonial era, APS members acknowledged the superiority of Chinese technology in areas of industry and agriculture, and at the same time sought ways to "introduce the produce and industry of the Chinese to this country," in Thomson's phrase.[4] After the completion of independence, with the elimination of much of the traditional foreign trade, APS researches about China were given additional impetus. As member Humphry Marshall, a botanist, explained in 1785, the importation and cultivation of foreign plants would relieve the United States from dependence on foreign nations. He singled out tea seedlings as an example of a foreign product which might be imported and cultivated in the southern United States.[5] In response to such expressed views, plus those of the Philadelphia Society for Promoting Agriculture, China traders, in the course of their voyages, assembled collections of Chinese plants and other Oriental natural history specimens, which were donated to Peale's Museum, to the Wagner Free Institute of Science, and to Pennsylvania Hospital, where they were studied. The *Empress of China* shipped back Shanghai roosters, from which the "Bucks County Chicken," now in abundance, was bred. By 1800, the APS was involved in the propagation of Chinese vetches and soybeans. By 1830, the Society was promoting sericulture and urging Congressional action conducive to the development of an American silk industry. In 1835, the APS bestowed membership upon Nathan Dunn for assembling a collection of Chinese agricultural specimens and other natural history relics that formed the nucleus of his "Chinese Museum," to be discussed later in this chapter. "None of our citizens," wrote his membership sponsors, "have shown a warmer desire to promote useful knowledge."[6]

In the area of architectural technology, and specifically the design of buildings and landscapes, Philadelphians exhibited the same admiration for, and imitation of, aspects of Chinese culture as they had in their study of Chinese agricultural products. In some cases, Chinese-style buildings were erected by China merchants themselves. Other edifices utilized ideas or goods which the businessmen had brought back.

Reference has already been made to Robert Morris' innovative practice of importing an entire set of home furnishings from China. Other Philadelphians did not stop at having just a few Chinese artifacts around the house. They had their buildings designed and constructed in the Chinese style, with chinoiserie inside and out. Five examples of such building styles in the Philadelphia area were Van Braam's "China Retreat," Croydon, Pa., 1796; John Markoe's summerhouse, Philadelphia, 1806, and John Latimer's, Wilmington, Del., 1838; Peter Browne's Philadelphia pagoda, 1828; and Nathan Dunn's "Chinese Cottage," Mt. Holly, N.J., 1832.

Van Braam's "China Retreat" was a landmark on the West Bank of the Delaware until its destruction in 1970. This trader's fondness for Chinese culture had developed during a fifteen-year residence in China in the employ of the Dutch East India Company, prior to his assumption of United States citizenship. His manor house had several Chinese features. The building was topped by a small pagoda, from the corners of which dangled silver wind bells. The fenestration was also Far Eastern: instead of sash or casement windows, the seven-foot broad voids were provided with dual panels, glazed with unprecedentedly large panes for that period, which slid back into wall pockets. Another feature of the new frame house was that the ceilings were seventeen and one-half feet high. They may have been designed in this fashion in order to accommodate Chinese wallpaper panels, which came in sixteen-foot lengths.[7]

The outstanding object on the interior was a seventeen-figure Chinese diorama which included humans, pagodas, rocks, bridges, ponds, streams, and trees. The artist William Birch, who prominently featured Van Braam's house in his *Country Seats of the United States,* described the diorama as the most beautiful set of Chinese ornaments he had ever seen.[8] In addition to the Chinese furnishings, Van Braam kept a library with about 2,000 drawings of China and its people. And, lest this environment still leave the visitor with only a vague image of China, Van Braam employed eight Chinese house servants, who constituted one of the earliest groups of Chinese immigrants to the United States. Van Braam's environmental milieu affected the Philadelphia publisher Moreau de Saint-Méry in the following way:

> The furniture, ornaments, everything at Mr. Van Braam's reminds us of China. It is impossible to avoid fancying ourselves in China, while surrounded at once by living Chinese, and by representations of their manners, their usages, their monuments, and their arts.[9]

The palatial milieu lasted for only two years. After suffering a series of financial reverses, Van Braam sold the property and moved to England. The fate of his eight Chinese servants is unknown.[10]

In addition to "China Retreat," several other, albeit less ambitious, attempts were made to employ Chinese designs in the Philadelphia region. Approximately ten miles from "China Retreat," across the Delaware River in Mount Holly, New Jersey, stood Nathan Dunn's "Chinese Cottage." In 1832, upon his return from China to Philadelphia, Dunn commissioned the architect John Notman to build him a country house in the Chinese style. Notman's creation was an eclectic structure whose Chinese elements included a striped, dipping roof over the entrance. Pendants, pointed arches, and two bulbous pinnacles capping the porch colonnettes may also have been Eastern in their inspiration. The nineteenth-century architectural critic A. J. Downing praised Dunn's innovative effort in creating a semi-oriental cottage in America, and featured a drawing of the building in an 1841 architectural treatise (see illustration). According to Downing, the inclusion of Chinese architectural motifs produced a delightful result "adapted to the American climate" and distinct in that one fixed, traditional style had not been followed.[11] The edifice, greatly remodeled, still stands in Mount Holly.

Moving back across the Delaware River to Philadelphia, the summerhouse behind the John Markoe residence offers an example of the usage of Chinese garden architecture. This small pavilion was designed by Benjamin Latrobe and built in 1806 in the block bounded by Market and Chestnut, Ninth and Tenth streets. Its flaring Chinese roof and entablature were supported by slender classic columns. Intricate Chinese-style latticework between the posts formed a back for the bench which encircled the interior of the structure. Later moved by Markoe's daughter to Mount Holly, the building was finally returned to Pennsylvania in 1947 to grace the Walter Jeffords estate in Glen Riddle.[12]

Some thirty years after the construction of the Markoe garden house, John Latimer, upon his return from the Orient, had a similar pavilion and Chinese garden furnishings incorporated into "Latimeria," his 142-acre estate near Wilmington, Delaware. Located just south of Philadelphia, the "Latimeria" garden house was octagonal, and was situated amid Chinese bird houses, a latticed pagoda with oval openings and double gates, and a squat, mushroom-topped circular bench. All of these articles may be seen today in the Winterthur Museum gardens.[13]

One final example of the use of Chinese architecture for recreational purposes in the Philadelphia area was the 100-foot high pagoda, complete with Chinese pavilion and garden, erected in Fairmount Park, Philadelphia, in 1828. This was the product of the imagination of Peter Browne, a dilettante whose tie with the China trade was that the pagoda's design was taken directly from *Designs of Chinese Buildings* by William Chambers, an Englishman who had toured China and made drawings in the 1740s. Although the plan for the tall structure has been attributed to both John Haviland and William Strickland, it is almost exactly a copy of a tower at Canton familiar to most foreign visitors and illustrated in Chambers' study. Browne's "Pagoda and Labyrinth Garden," as the complex was known, in all probability combined refreshment facilities and botanical displays with some sort of entertainment.[14]

Browne's edifice, like the others, represents the deliberate adaptation of an aspect of Chinese culture for a positive purpose in early America. The fact that early Americans chose to decorate in this fashion indicates that they felt at ease with Chinese culture.

Clearly, were that culture something looked down upon, one would not have wanted to be deluged with artifacts and designs from it. The utilization of architectural motifs, like the purchase of standard-issue Chinese decorative goods, entailed both an aesthetic and utilitarian appreciation.

The Interpretation of China in Museums and Published Scholarship

Another indication of the early Philadelphia opinion of China was the image conveyed in museum displays and published scholarship.

Of all the individuals examined thus far, Nathan Dunn was an outstanding example of a nineteenth-century Philadelphian who consciously sought to promote positive attitudes toward the Celestials. Like the colonial intellectual Charles Thomson before him, Dunn's interest in China flowed from his broader interests in industry and education. He was distinguished for his philanthropic role in the establishment of the Quaker college, Haverford, and for his aid to other Philadelphia institutions: the APS, the Academy of Natural Sciences, and the Laurel Hill Cemetery. When he was nominated for membership in the APS in 1835, his sponsors advised the Society that "few persons have shown deeper interest in promoting the prosperity of our public institutions literary and benevolent than Mr. Dunn."[15]

Dunn's first project, as noted, was similar to that of other Philadelphians: the creation of a Chinese-style mansion on American shores. After finishing his dwelling, Dunn embarked upon an undertaking which had even greater impact on introducing Chinese culture in the Philadelphia region. The "Chinese Museum," in Philadelphia at Ninth and George (now Sansom) streets, was open to the public from 1839 to 1842, and contained artifacts which Dunn and his fellow Philadelphian William Wood had assembled in China over a period of nine years. Visitors entered through richly carved wooden gates flanked by two enormous Chinese lanterns. Lanterns and silk banners hung from the ceiling. Ten huge exhibit cases displayed life-size clay figurines which had been modeled in China and dressed in full costume representing scenes from everyday Chinese life: mandarins of rank, scholars in their study, ladies preparing their toilet, actors and jugglers on a stage, a silk merchant in his shop, and agricultural laborers with a water buffalo pulling a plough. A furnished Chinese room contained model temples, boats, summerhouses, bridges, and a demonstration on the manufacture of ceramics. There was a total of 1,200 Chinese art and craft objects and natural history specimens. Those visitors with sufficient interest and strength could also view several hundred paintings by Chinese artists working for the export trade, including several of the largest port paintings ever executed, which were fully nine feet long and five feet high. More than 100,000 Americans visited "The Chinese Collection in Philadelphia," and 50,000 copies of the *Descriptive Catalogue* were sold in the first few months of the exhibit.[16]

The importance of Dunn's museum as a vehicle for introducing many thousands of Americans to the positive features of Chinese culture was noted by many contemporaries. Enoch Wines, the Philadelphia social reformer and minister, observed that the collection was the "richest deposit of curiosities from the Celestial Empire" in the Western world. There were only three museums even approximately comparable to Dunn's in the world at the time—in The Hague, in London, and in Salem, Massachusetts. The Dutch Chinese collection was much smaller than Dunn's, and the British East India Company display in London included non-Chinese artifacts from India, as did the Salem exhibit. According to Wines, after examining this extraordinary collection, one could gain a realization of the "characteristic intelligence and natural customs of the Chinese." Wines advised that

> Dunn, in the collection he now offers to public examination, has done more than any other man to rectify prevalent errors and disseminate true information concerning a nation every way worthy to be studied by the economist who searches into the principles of national prosperity and stability.[17]

Benjamin Silliman, the Yale scientist, appraised Dunn's museum much in the way Wines had. After viewing the display, Silliman wrote that "if an architect desires to examine his science in China, he will find models of ancient and majestic bridges [and] the Great Wall; the artist, paintings admirably colored; the mercer, rich silks; the porcelain manufacturer, the grand originals of his art." Silliman hoped that the museum would counteract the negative images of eighteenth-century China conveyed to the public in some accounts. His appraisal of Dunn's effort was published in his own *American Journal of Science and Arts* in January 1839. It was excerpted in Washington's *Niles' National Register* the following month and appeared in book form in Philadelphia in 1841. James Buckingham, a British visitor, wrote that the museum aided "the increase of new information and the correction of many old errors." He included an entire chapter on the museum in his American travelogue.[19]

There is evidence that Dunn's museum disturbed those Americans harboring negative views of the Chinese. Elijah Bridgman, the American missionary in China, after reading Wines' favorable review of Dunn's exhibit, commented that the show was "a little too favorable" with respect to the "principles of the Chinese." Bridgman cited the "common honesty of the people" as an example of Dunn's exaggeration. Bridgman's commentary was apparently the nearest thing to negative criticism which Dunn's display received. Even it corroborated the overwhelmingly positive nature of the information about China which Dunn was communicating to Americans.[20]

Dunn, like Van Braam before him, underwent financial reverses after returning to the United States from China. Both he and his collection moved to London in 1841. But his was not the last display of chinoiserie that Philadelphia would see. In 1847, yet another Chinese Museum, established by John Peters, a member of the Caleb Cushing diplomatic expedition to China, was set up in Philadelphia. Said to provide an "extensive view of the Central Flowery Nation," Peters' museum appears to have been even larger than Dunn's, containing sixty full-size figures to his fifty-three. The outstanding object was a representation of the Tao Kwang Emperor in full court dress with mandarins of the first six ranks.[21]

While the evidence of museums, and the commentary they elicited, has given some notion of the regard in which Chinese culture was held in early Philadelphia, additional published evidence can be introduced to show attitudes toward the Chinese people and their culture. This last body of evidence of scholarship—completed in nineteenth-century Philadelphia—was also a continuation of research begun in the Colonial period.

In the nineteenth century, APS Secretary Peter Duponceau sustained the work begun by the circle of colonial scholars headed by Charles Thomson. Duponceau's specialty was linguistics, and he was possibly the first American academic to scientifically analyze the Chinese language, as he had done with American Indian dialects. He drew upon eyewitness accounts furnished by China traders and engaged in an active correspondence with European sinologists. His major scholarly contribution, published by the APS in 1838, was his observation of the ready comprehensibility of the written Chinese character among diverse Asiatic cultures. He noted the value of the Chinese language as a lingua franca unifying peoples who comprised between one-quarter and one-third of the world's population. And, far from suggesting Chinese inferiority, Duponceau stressed in his extensive writings the complexity and highly evolved state of the Chinese written medium.[22]

The writings on China of Philadelphian Robert Waln, Jr., constituted perhaps the most forceful early American assertion of the positive features of Chinese society, and were perhaps the most earnest
early American effort to eradicate any anti-Chinese bias. Clifton Phillips, in his analysis of early American attitudes toward paganism,
considered Waln America's "first Sinologist" because of the research
this merchant conducted while trading in China during the years
1819–20, and his extensive publication on the subject in the 1820s,
prior to that of Duponceau. Waln asserted in his 475-page history of
China that accounts by European Catholic missionaries, in particular,
were "so confused by the credulity and superstition of the narrators it
would be almost impracticable to obtain from them a proper insight
into the character and condition of the Chinese nation."[23] Waln
found especially libelous the missionary "descriptions" of infanticide
in China which they had not observed firsthand. He argued on the
basis of his research in both China and the United States that while
the Chinese might have engaged in infanticide during conditions of
extreme hardship, such as famine, the practice occurred with no
greater frequency in China than under similarly harsh conditions in
Christian countries. The existence of Chinese government-funded
Foundling Hospitals, which he had personally observed in Canton,
rendered the missionary charge of government-sponsored infanticide
highly implausible. Waln pointed to the poor record of missionaries
in making Chinese converts. He suggested that the omission of positive features of Chinese society, such as Foundling Hospitals, from
missionary accounts reflected a deliberate intent to depict Chinese
culture as a particularly vicious version of heathen barbarism, even if
such an image was contrary to fact. He suggested that missionary
accounts which described the numbers of infants they had rescued
from the "pit of death" were self-serving reports designed to elicit
financial support in Western countries.[24]

In addition to the writings of Waln and Duponceau, Van Braam,
the only American to have visited the interior regions of China before
1844, published an account of his travels in which he emphasized
positive and progressive features of Confucianism, such as the social
responsibilities which Chinese owed to each other. These aspects of
Chinese religion were rarely if ever noted by anti-Chinese pundits of
the *Port Folio* variety. Because of his travel and research work in
China, Van Braam was elected to the APS in 1797, after the first
volume of his travelogue was published in Philadelphia.[25]

In concluding, we may once again ask what the varied types of
evidence from Philadelphia's China trade indicate concerning the
possibility of a strongly prejudicial, anti-Chinese bias in early Amer-

ica. The preceding evidence of material culture, literature, and events would tend to indicate that there was no widespread prejudice. In early post-Revolutionary Philadelphia, on even a larger scale than in Colonial Philadelphia, Chinese crafts, motifs, and ideas were esteemed by traders, men of letters, and a broad public for their aesthetic worth as well as for their utility. The creativity and skill of the Chinese were acknowledged as being superior to those of early Americans in areas of agriculture, architecture, landscaping, and fine arts, as well as in the manufacture of textiles, ceramics, and artistic reproductions. While the practicality, inexpensiveness, and high quality of Chinese goods tendered a welcome profit to the importer, at the same time both trader and consumer frequently expressed an admiration for the Chinese aesthetic. Positive notions about Chinese culture were disseminated to a broad public through the promotional activities of organizations like the APS; in the writings of Thomson, Ledyard, Morris, Shaw, Swift, Randall, Moreau de Saint-Méry, Duponceau, Van Braam, Wines, Silliman, Robert Waln, Jr., and Girard; and in the public displays created by Dunn and Peters. The displays were a particularly efficacious device for communicating ideas in an era before the introduction of mass media, and they elicited a positive response from critics and the public at large.

In summation, if we make the assumption of a basic selectivity possessed by individuals, it seems safe to conclude that most early Philadelphians would have differentiated between those features of China which they did not like, such as a rampaging mob or venal civil servants, and the more positive aspects of Chinese civilization. An American might have reacted in one manner to a mandarin, an official of the Chinese governing elite, and quite differently to an artisan he might engage for some gold filigree work or automated toys. The attitudes of the overwhelming majority of early Philadelphians who took an interest in the Chinese could not be categorized as "racist," and might better be described as entrepreneurial, cordial, and tolerant.

One final question which may be reintroduced is, if we are to overlook a heritage of anti-Oriental prejudice, how can one account for the occurrence of militant anti-Orientalism and Chinese exclusion, particularly in the American West? What of the suggestion by Hilary Conroy and T. Scott Miyakawa, concerning Japanese-Americans, that a "racist heritage" with strong emotional overtones may have justified in the minds of many Americans the indignities and inequalities deliberately imposed on Asian immigrants and Asian Americans?[26]

It has not been the objective of this study to furnish explanations for such events, other than to suggest that this behavior did not emanate in any substantial measure from the influence of the early China trade. It should, however, be noted that at least three other scholars who have recently examined the question of anti-Orientalism have been able to account for the phenomenon without reference to a heritage of anti-Orientalism transmitted from the East Coast. Luther Spoehr, in his 1973 study, reiterated Edward Graham's suggestion that Oriental exclusion and discrimination were peculiar expressions of popular discontent at a particularly tension-ridden juncture in Western history. Robert Heizer and Alan Almquist advanced the view that "in the absence of blacks the anti-Negro sentiments [of Californians] were applied to Chinese." Alexander Saxton asserted that the "main dynamic" for the anti-Chinese movement came from the "historic experience with blacks and slavery."[27]

While these explanations may or may not be valid, there does appear to be one connection between early Sino-American relations and subsequent anti-Orientalism. The fundamentally harmonious personal relations between Americans and Chinese, which had slowly evolved in the course of two hundred years of trading together over great distances, without the aid of modern means of transportation and communication, were done severe damage by the rise of American sentiment against Chinese immigration. As Edward Graham has written, these acts resulted in an erosion of popular faith in the significance of the Sino-American nexus, a concept which was painstakingly nurtured by Philadelphia merchants and intellectuals. In 1860, as the erosion of the nexus was developing, John Latimer, who had been out of the China trade for nearly thirty years, and who had retired with his chinoiserie to his Delaware estate, reminisced over the course of the Sino-American relations that he and his ancestors had participated in for nearly a century. Latimer still favorably recalled the old China trade, and attested that "the trade conducted at Canton on common sense principles was better for the Chinese, better for the foreigners, more conducive to peace and success than all that has been gained otherwise."[29]

Sino-American relations in the earlier period had not been free of conflict. However, they were certainly not thus free in 1860. Nor, it can be argued, have they ever been significantly improved over the complex pattern of tense governmental relations and smooth trade and personal relations manifested in Philadelphia's old China trade.

Chinese "varnish tree"

Notes

The following abbreviations are used throughout the Notes and Bibliography:

APS   The American Philosophical Society

APSL   The American Philosophical Society Library, Philadelphia

CR   *The Chinese Repository* (Canton, 1832–51)

DL   Nathan Dunn Letterbooks, 1829–38, G. W. Blunt White Library Manuscript Collection, Mystic Seaport, Mystic, Connecticut

EIHC   *Historical Collections of the Essex Institute*

FMC   *The Foreign Missionary Chronicle*

HSP   The Historical Society of Pennsylvania, Philadelphia

INA   The Archives and Historical Collection of the Insurance Company of North America, Philadelphia

JB   The James Bancker Papers, American Philosophical Society Library, Philadelphia

LC   The Library Company of Philadelphia

MH   *The Missionary Herald*

MHS   The Massachusetts Historical Society, Boston

NYHS   New-York Historical Society

PH   *Pennsylvania History*

PHR   *The Pacific Historical Review*

PMHB   *The Pennsylvania Magazine of History and Biography*

SG   Stephen Girard. All correspondence to or from Girard will, unless otherwise specified, be understood to have come from Stephen Girard Papers, Estate of Stephen Girard, dec'd, Philadelphia, Pennsylvania.

TAPS   *Transactions of the American Philosophical Society*

WP   Waln Family Papers, Library Company of Philadelphia

Chapter 1

1. Adam Smith, *An Inquiry Into the Nature and Causes of the Wealth of Nations*, I (London: printed for W. Strahan, 1776), p. 87, quoted in *The American Apollo* 1 (January 20, 1792), 21.

2. An inventory of John Latimer's personal effects noted the Chinese goods described, and particularly three Chinese paintings, artists unspecified, all showing Canton merchant residences. In one, the scene is peaceful. In another, the buildings are being consumed by fire and the Chinese are fleeing. In the last, smoke is rising from embers of the homes. The American flag probably flew from the U.S. Consulate. These items were moved from 359 Walnut to Latimer's Wilmington, Delaware, estate in the late 1830s. "Colonial Homes of Wilmington," *Every Evening* (Wilmington), December 13, 1913, p. 14.

3. [Carl Crossman], *An Exhibition and Sale of Paintings and Objects of the China Trade, October 20–November 21, 1969* (brochure), Childs Gallery, Boston.

4. The journalist Freeman Hunt observed that Chinese cinnamon was "the only kind used in the United States, the real cinnamon from Ceylon, such as is used in London, by the great families, coming too high for American use. It is ground up and sold as cinnamon by all the grocers in the United States." Hunt, *Lives of American Merchants*, I (New York: Office of Hunt's Merchant's Magazine, 1856), p. 40.

5. H. A. Crosby Forbes, "The American Vision of Cathay," in *Nineteenth Annual Washington Antiques Show/1974* (catalogue), p. 53.

6. On American historians' traditional aversion for non-Western history, see Jack Greene, "The 'New History': From Top to Bottom," *New York Times*, January 8, 1975.

7. Philadelphia's China trade received some attention in biographies of the trade's participants, such as John Latimer, John Barry, Stephen Girard, Andreas Van Braam, Nathan Dunn, Robert Morris, Elisha Kane, and Thomas Truxton. Charles Hummel, "John Richardson Latimer Comments on the American Scene," *Delaware History* 6 (September 1955), 267–87; Joan Thill, "A Delawarean in the Celestial Empire," unpublished M.A. thesis, University of Delaware, 1973; William Clark, *Gallant John Barry* (New York: Macmillan, 1938); Harry Wildes, *Lonely Midas* (New York: Farrar & Rinehart, 1943); George Loehr, "A. E. Van Braam Houckgeest, The First American at the Court of China," *Princeton University Library Chronicle* 15, no. 4 (Summer 1954), 179–93; Arthur Hummel, "Nathan Dunn," *Quaker History* 59, no. 1 (Spring 1970), 34–39; Ellis Oberholtzer, *Robert Morris. Patriot and*

Financier (New York: Macmillan, 1903); George Corner, *Doctor Kane of the Arctic Seas* (Philadelphia: Temple University Press, 1972); Eugene Ferguson, *Truxton of the Constellation* (Baltimore: Johns Hopkins University Press, 1956).

8. Helen Klopfer, "Statistics of the Foreign Trade of Philadelphia, 1700–1860," unpublished M.S., Ph.D. dissertation, University of Pennsylvania, 1936; Marion Brewington, "Maritime Philadelphia; 1609–1837," *PMHB* 63, no. 2 (April 1939), 93–117.

9. Ann White, "The China Trade From Philadelphia, 1785–1820," unpublished M.A. research paper, University of Pennsylvania, 1962.

10. Hilary Conroy and T. Scott Miyakawa, *East Across the Pacific. Historical & Sociological Studies of Japanese Immigration & Assimilation* (Santa Barbara, Calif.: American Bibliographical Center Clio Press, 1972), p. xi.

11. Kenneth Latourette, *The History of Early Relations Between the United States and China* (New Haven: Yale University Press, 1917), p. 124; Tyler Dennett, *Americans in East Asia* (New York: Macmillan, 1922), p. 61; Harold Isaacs, *Scratches on Our Minds. American Images of China and India* (New York: John Day, 1958), pp. 70–71; Edward Graham, "American Ideas of a Special Relationship with China, 1784–1900," unpublished Ph.D. dissertation, Harvard University, 1968, summary, n.p.

12. Stuart Creighton Miller, *The Unwelcome Immigrant. The American Image of the Chinese, 1785–1882* (Berkeley: University of California Press, 1969), p. 11. This was a revision of his Ph.D. dissertation, "The Chinese Image in the Eastern United States, 1785–1882," Columbia University, 1966.

13. Miller, *Immigrant,* p. 192. See also his article: "An East Coast Perspective to Chinese Exclusion, 1852–1882," *Historian* 33 (February 1971), 183–201, which concluded that "cultural, racial, and medical fears of national dimensions better explain Chinese exclusion than does a narrow California conspiracy. Certainly, the tail could not have wagged a dog that was less than willing to be wagged." On the traditional explanation for exclusion see: Mary Coolidge, *Chinese Immigration* (New York: Henry Holt, 1919); Foster Rhea Dulles, *China and America* (Princeton: Princeton University Press, 1946).

Full names of authors and full titles of works cited by surname and short title will be found in the Bibliography with complete facts of publication.

14. Hosea Morse, *The Gilds of China* (London: Longmans, 1933), p. 88.

15. Jonathan Goldstein, "The China Trade From Philadelphia, 1682–1846: A Study of Inter-regional Commerce and Cultural Interaction," Ph.D. dissertation, University of Pennsylvania, 1973, Chapter 1, lists names of Philadelphians who lived in China, and their length of residence.

16. Jesse Lemisch, "Jack Tar in the Streets: Merchant Seamen in the Politics of Revolutionary America," *William and Mary Quarterly,* 3d ser., 14, no. 3 (July 1968), 373–407.

Chapter 2

1. Charles Thomson, entry, January 1, 1768, First Minute Book, American Society, APSL; Charles Thomson, "Preface," *TAPS* 1 (January 1769–January 1771), vii.

2. Thomas C. Cochran, *Basic History of American Business,* 2d ed. (Princeton: Van Nostrand, 1968), p. 28.

3. Thomas La Fargue, "Some Early Chinese Visitors to the United States," *T'ien Hsia Monthly* 11 (October–November 1940), 129.

4. "Registers Granted at the Port of Philadelphia in the Quarter ending 5th January 1775," *PMHB* 39, no. 2 (1915), 93; On the Latimers, see James Scharf, *History of Delaware 1609–1888,* II (Philadelphia: L. J. Richards 1888), p. 735; John Campbell, *History of the Society of the Friendly Sons of Saint Patrick* (Philadelphia: Hibernian Society, 1892), pp. 119–20; *Biographical and Genealogical History of the State of Delaware,* II (Chambersburg, Pa.: J. M. Runk, 1899), p. 140; Samuel Small, *Genealogical Records of George Small* (Philadelphia: J. B. Lippincott, 1905), pp. 142–43, 161–68. On the Walns and Donnaldsons, see Richard Waln, Jr., Walnford Mill Accounts, 1772, HSP; Letters of John, Richard, and Edward Donnaldson, 1700–1850, *passim,* Montgomery County Historical Society, Norristown, Pa.; (Stephen Winslow), *Biographies of Successful Philadelphia Merchants* (Philadelphia: James K. Simon, 1864), pp. 129–32.

5. Robert East, *Business Enterprise in the American Revolutionary Era* (New York: Columbia University Press, 1938), pp. 126–48; Klopfer, "Statistics," p. 208.

6. James Livingood, *The Philadelphia-Baltimore Trade Rivalry* (Harrisburg: Pennsylvania Historical and Museum Commission, 1947), p. iii; Sara Farris, "Wilmington's Maritime Commerce, 1775–1807," *Delaware History* 14, no. 1 (April 1970), 22–51.

7. *Pennsylvania Chronicle,* March 7, 1768.

8. William Smith, "A Short Account of the Present State of the College," *Universal Asylum and Columbian Magazine* 5 (1790), 275.

9. Charles Thomson, entry, January 1, 1768, First Minute Book; Thomson, "Preface," vii.

10. Thomson, "Preface," iii–xviii. "Whisk" may be a reference to "broom-corn millet," a plant that was native to the East Indies. Its panicles were used for making brooms and brushes. It is also referred to as *sorghum vulgare* and *panicum miliaceum.* L. H. Bailey and Ethel Bailey, *Hortus* (New York: Macmillan, 1935), p. 441; *The Compact Edition of the Oxford English Dictionary* (1971), vol. 1, p. 283; vol. 2, p. 3762. Letters, Peter Duponceau to John Bailey, April 16, 22, 1830, Washburn Papers, MHS; Edwin Conklin, "The American Philosophical Society and the Founders of Our Government," *PH* 4, no. 4 (1937), 238.

11. Benjamin Rush, "Observation [on] the Black Color of the Negroes," *TAPS* 4 (1779), 289–97.

12. William Stanton, *The Leopard's Spots: Scientific Attitudes Toward Race in America* (Chicago: University of Chicago Press, 1960), p. viii; Winthrop Jordan, *White Over Black* (Baltimore: Penguin Books, 1969), pp. 242, 305–6.

13. Robert Waln, Jr., "Miscellanies Vol. 5," 1820, Waln Family Papers, Library Company of Philadelphia; Rodris Roth, *Tea Drinking in 18th-Century America* (Washington: Smithsonian Institution, 1961), p. 63; B. Sprague Allen, *Tides in English Taste (1619–1800),* I (New York: Pageant Books, 1958), p. 234. See also Hugh Honour, *Chinoiserie: The Vision of Cathay* (London: John Murray, 1961), p. 203.

14. Claude Robin, *Nouveau Voyage dans l'Amérique 1781* (Philadelphia:

Moutard, 1782), p. 19; Samuel Wharton, "Observations on Consumption of Teas in North America," written in London, January 19, 1773, in *PMHB* 25, no. 1 (1901), 139–41; Gideon Nye, "American Commerce with China," *The Far East* (Shanghai), n.s., 4 (January 1878), 16.

15. Benjamin Labaree, *The Boston Tea Party* (New York: Oxford University Press, 1964), p. 331. Labaree's figures were taken from customs 3/50–/74, British Public Record Office. Corroborating statistics, taken from an abstract prepared in the Office of the Inspector of Imports and Exports, appear in Edward Channing, *A History of the United States,* III (New York: Macmillan, 1916), p. 128. Labaree offers a comprehensive account of the entire tea trade in Colonial America.

16. Letters: John Waddell to Sayre and Wharton, May 6, 27; June 7, 28; September 20, 1756, Wharton Correspondence, 1679–1759, HSP; Thomas Wharton to Robert Moulder, July 2, 1756; to John Waddell, July 3 and 7, August 5, 20, and 26, 1756—Wharton Letterbook, 1752–59, HSP; Thomas Riché to Jacob van Zand, August 13, 1755—Riché Letterbooks, 1750–71, HSP; John Kidd to Rawlinson and Davidson, September 21, 1756—Kidd Letterbooks, 1749–63, HSP. Arthur Jensen, "The Maritime Commerce of Colonial Philadelphia," unpublished Ph.D. dissertation, University of Wisconsin, 1954, p. 280.

17. Letters: Richard Waln to William Hales, September 14, 1771—Waln Letterbook, 1766–99, HSP; Willing and Morris to Mayne, Burn, and Mayne, May 6, 1756—Willing Letterbooks, 1754–61, HSP; Kidd to Rawlinson and Davidson, January 28, 1757.

18. Jensen, "Commerce," p. 280; Thomas Taylor, "Philadelphia's Counterpart of the Boston Tea Party," *Bulletin of the Friends' Historical Society of Philadelphia* 2 (November 1908), 88–99; Sidney Fisher, *True History of the Revolution* (Philadelphia: Lippincott, 1902), p. 407.

19. Letter: Daniel Roberdeau to Cruger and Gouverneur, November 13, 1764, Roberdeau Letterbook, 1764–71, HSP; Jensen, "Commerce," p. 295.

20. Letter: Samuel Wharton to George Read, February 19, 1770, Dreer Collection, n.s., HSP. Wharton was apparently referring not only to the tea tax, but to other Parliamentary legislation as well.

21. Samuel Wharton, "Observations," pp. 139–41.

22. Samuel Wharton, "Observations," pp. 139–41.

23. *Pennsylvania Packet,* January 3, 1774; anonymous note to Abel James and Henry Drinker, Fall 1773, in *PMHB* 15 (1891), 389–90; Jensen, "Commerce," p. 398; Frank Leach, "The Philadelphia of Our Ancestors. Old Philadelphia Families. Wharton," *North American,* July 7, 1907.

24. Letters: Thomas Riché to George Clifford, September 18, 1762; to Q. Hodshon, October 7, 1762—Riché Letterbooks, 1750–71. Benjamin Franklin, *The Autobiography of Benjamin Franklin,* ed. by Leonard Labaree, Ralph Ketcham, Helene Boatfield, and Helene Fineman (New Haven: Yale University Press, 1964), p. 145.

25. Benjamin Franklin to Deborah Franklin, February 19, 1758, in *The Papers of Benjamin Franklin,* ed. by Leonard Labaree, VI (New Haven: Yale University Press, 1963), p. 381.

26. Shards from Franklin's trash pit are described in the Franklin Court Project's archaeological report. Barbara Liggett, *Archaeology at Franklin's*

Court (Harrisburg, Pa.: McFarland, 1973). On domestic manufacture, see: Graham Hood, *Bonnin and Morris of Philadelphia: The First American Porcelain Factory, 1770–1772* (Chapel Hill: University of North Carolina Press, 1972); John Watson, *Annals of Philadelphia and Pennsylvania*, II (Philadelphia: Carey & Hart, 1844), p. 272.

27. F. Porter Smith, *Chinese Materia Medica*, revised by G. A. Stuart (Shanghai: American Presbyterian Mission Press, 1911), pp. 301–2. The most comprehensive single source on the use and marketing of ginseng within China is Van Symons, "The Ch'ing Ginseng Monopoly," unpublished Ph.D. dissertation, Brown University, 1975. See also William Constable, "Two Notes on Ginseng," ca. 1787, New York Public Library, Constable-Pierrepont Collection; Letter: Thomas Randall to Alexander Hamilton, August 14, 1791, in *The Industrial and Commercial Correspondence of Alexander Hamilton*, ed. by Arthur Cole (Chicago: A. W. Shaw Company, 1928), p. 132; J. Dyer Ball, *Things Chinese* (London: Sampson Low, Marston and Company, 1900), p. 268; Ulysses Hendrick, *A History of Agriculture in the State of New York* (Albany: New York State Agricultural Society, 1933), pp. 136–37; Brendan Jones, "Ginseng, Seoul's Oldest Export," *New York Times*, March 14, 1971.

28. William Griffis, *Corea. The Hermit Nation* (New York: Scribner, 1882), pp. 388–89.

29. On Jesuits and the colonial ginseng trade, see Pierre Jartoux, "Lettre du Père [*sic*] Jartoux . . . a Pekin, le 12. d'Avril 1711," *Lettres Edifiantes et Curieuses*, X (Paris: Jean Barbou, 1713), pp. 159–85; and Joseph Lafitau, *Mémoire . . . Concernant . . . Gin-seng* (Montréal: Typographie de Senecal, 1858). Both Jartoux and Lafitau include drawings of the ginseng plant. The 1858 printing of Lafitau's 1718 memoir includes a preface entitled: "Le Père Lafitau et le Gin-seng." See also Joseph Lafitau, *Moeurs des Sauvages Amériquains*, II (Paris: Saugrain et Hochereau, 1724), pp. 141–42; Mark Catesby, *Natural History of Carolina, Florida, and the Bahama Islands*, II (London: Printed at the expense of the author, 1743), p. 16 of appendix; Justin Winsor, *Narrative and Critical History of America*, IV (Boston: Houghton Mifflin, 1886), p. 289; Camille de Rochemonteix, *Les Jésuites et la Nouvelle-France au XVIIe Siècle*, III (Paris: Letouzey et Ané, 1896), pp. 385–86; Reuben Thwaites, *Jesuit Relations and Allied Documents* (Cleveland: Burrows Brothers, 1896–1901), LXVII, p. 333; LXXI, p. 347; Latourette, *Relations*, p. 10.

30. Watson, *Annals*, II, p. 427.

31. Letter: James Pemberton to John Pemberton, December 18, 1752, Pemberton Papers, VIII, 112, HSP; William Speer, *The Oldest and the Newest Empire* (Hartford: S. S. Scranton, 1870), p. 410.

32. David MacPherson, *Annals of Commerce*, III (London: Nichols and Son et al., 1805), p. 572; R. Fenton Duvall, "Philadelphia's Maritime Commerce with the British Empire, 1783–1789," unpublished Ph.D. dissertation, University of Pennsylvania, 1960, p. 414.

33. For primary source material on Philadelphians' search for a northwest route to China see Thomas Jefferys, *The Great Probability of a Northwest Passage* (London: Thomas Jefferys, 1768). This work contains an appendix entitled: "An Account of Labrador Being an Extract from a Journal of a Voyage made from Philadelphia in 1753." The authorship of the "Appendix" has been attributed to Captain Swain of the *Argo* by Harold Eavenson

in *Two Early Works on Arctic Exploration* (Pittsburgh: no publisher cited, 1946). See also Berta Solis-Cohen, "Philadelphia's Expeditions to Labrador," *PH* 19 (April 1952), 150–62; Edwin Balch, "Arctic Expeditions Sent From the American Colonies," *PMHB* 31, no. 4 (1970), 419–28; Carl Bridenbaugh, *Cities in Revolt. Urban Life in America 1743–1776* (New York: Knopf, 1955), p. 202; Bridenbaugh and Bridenbaugh, *Rebels,* p. 329.

Chapter 3

1. Philip Freneau, "On the First American Ship That Explored the Route to CHINA, and the EAST-INDIES, After the Revolution," *Poems Written Between the Years 1768 & 1794* (Monmouth, N.J.: At the Press of the Author, 1795), p. 291.

2. The voyage of the ship *United States* to India is discussed later in this chapter. On diplomatic conditions in the Orient and West Indies, see Letter: Parish & Co. to Stephen Girard, June 30, 1815, Stephen Girard Papers, Estate of Stephen Girard, Philadelphia, Pennsylvania, on microfilm in American Philosophical Society Library, Philadelphia. All correspondence to or from Girard will be understood to have come from this collection, unless otherwise indicated. See also Samuel Bemis, *Jay's Treaty* (New Haven: Yale University Press, 1962), pp. 469–71; Holden Furber, "The Beginnings of American Trade with India, 1784–1812," *New England Quarterly* 11 (June 1938), 240–65; Albert Gares, "Stephen Girard's West India Trade, 1789–1812," unpublished Ed.D. dissertation, Temple University, 1947, pp. 72–88; Samuel Bemis, *A Diplomatic History of the United States* (New York: Holt, 1951), pp. 100–102.

3. John Ledyard, *A Journal of Captain Cook's Last Voyage* (Hartford: Nathaniel Patten, 1783); Richard Van Alstyne, *The Rising American Empire* (New York: Oxford University Press, 1960), p. 124.

4. By a Yankee, *The Adventures of a Yankee; or the Singular Life of John Ledyard* (Boston: Carter, Hendee, and Babcock, 1831), p. 64; Jared Sparks, *Life of John Ledyard, the American Traveller* (Boston: Charles C. Little and James Brown, 1847), p. 175; Samuel Shaw, *The Journals of Mayor Samuel Shaw. The First American Consul at Canton,* ed. by Josiah Quincy (Boston: Wm. Crosby and H. P. Nichols, 1847), p. 133; Clarence Ver Steeg, "Financing and Outfitting the First United States Ship to China," *PHR* 22 (February 1953), 5–6.

5. Primary source material on the *Empress'* 1784 voyage to China includes Shaw, *Journals;* the "Receit Book, F. Molineux for Account of Captain Green," Canton, 1784 and 1786, University of Pennsylvania Library Rare Book Collection, Philadelphia; and the John Green Papers, property of the Thibault family, Saint David's, Pa. The Molineux item is an account kept on the first *Empress* voyage (Canton, 1784) and on the second voyage (Canton, 1786). The Green papers consist of miscellaneous *Empress* material, including the ship's manifest from its first China voyage. HSP owns a Chinese watercolor painting of the vessel in Chinese waters. The painting is part of a mother-of-pearl Chinese fan (see cover illustration). Secondary material on the first voyage includes Versteeg, "Financing," and William Fairburn, *Merchant Sail,* I (Center Lovell, Me.: Fairburn Marine Educational Foundation,

1945–55), pp. 497–98. See also Robert Morris to John Jay, November 27, 1783, in *The Correspondence and Public Papers of John Jay,* ed. by Henry Johnston, III (New York: Putnam, 1891), p. 97.

6. Ann White, "The Hong Merchants of Canton," unpublished Ph.D. dissertation, University of Pennsylvania, 1968, pp. 36–82; Hosea Morse, *The Chronicles of the East India Company Trading to China, 1635–1834,* V (Oxford: Oxford University Press, 1926), pp. 56–93; W. E. Cheong, "Trade and Finance in China, 1784–1834. A Reappraisal," *Business History* (Liverpool) 7, no. 1 (January 1965), 34–38. The name *kung-hang* is pronounced the same in both Mandarin and Cantonese. It is sometimes confused with *kuan-hang* (Mandarin) or *kun-hang* (Cantonese), which also means a government *hang* or company, but is a general term for such organizations. The members of the cohong were called *kuan-shang,* "official merchants."

7. Letters: Randall to Alexander Hamilton, August 14, 1791 in *Hamilton,* ed. Cole; Samuel Shaw to Winthrop Sargeant, November 19, 1785, Society Miscellaneous Collection, HSP.

8. "Receit Book, F. Molineux," University of Pennsylvania Library; Henry Forbes, John Kernan, and Ruth Wilkins, *Chinese Export Silver* (Milton, Mass.: Museum of the American China Trade, 1975); East, *Business,* pp. 254–55.

9. Letter: John White Swift to John Swift, December 3, 1787, *PMHB* 9, no. 4 (1885), 485.

10. Shaw, *Journals,* p. 183. For additional expressions in mercantile correspondence of the commercial importance of Morris' venture, see Letters: John Girard to SG, May 4, 1784; Alexander Nesbitt to Walter Stewart, May 7, 1785, Papers of Stewart, Nesbitt & Co., Mariner's Museum Library, Newport News, Virginia. See also Letter: Richard Henry Lee to James Madison, May 30, 1785, in *The Letters of Richard Henry Lee,* ed. by James Ballagh, II (New York: Macmillan, 1914), p. 366.

11. *Massachusetts Centinel* (Boston), May 18, 1785. The following newspapers also carried information about the *Empress'* successful completion of its first voyage: *Daily Advertiser* (New York), May 16, 1785; *New York Packet,* May 16, 1785; *Providence Gazette,* May 18, 1785; *Newport Mercury,* May 21, 1785; *Freeman's Journal* (Philadelphia), June 22, 1785; *Delaware Gazette* (Wilmington), January 18, 1786.

12. *Pennsylvania Packet* (Philadelphia), May 16, 1785.

13. Freneau, "On the First Ship," *Poems,* p. 291; Helen Augur, *Passage to Glory: John Ledyard's America* (Garden City, N.Y.: Doubleday, 1946), pp. 140–41.

14. Letters: Samuel Shaw to John Jay, May 19, 1785, in *The American Museum* 1 (March 1787), 194–97; to Jay, January 1789, in Shaw, *Journals,* pp. 350–51; Shaw, "Remarks on the Commerce of America with China," *The American Museum* 7 (March 1790), 126–28.

15. Statistics were taken at Canton, from the records of the American Consulate. Stateside figures were inaccurate, since many United States ships cleared American ports destined for China but never got there; many cleared destined for other ports, yet wound up in Canton. Robert Waln, Jr., "Abstracts of Philada Trade to Canton"; "Memo Book, Canton, September 1819 to January 1820," p. 52, WP; J[eremiah] Reynolds, *Voyage of the United States Frigate Potomac* (New York: Harper, 1835), p. 380.

16. Letter: SG to Richard Parish, March 29, 1817. Robert Waln, Sr.,

entry for April 19, 1819, Letterbook, 1815–19, WP; Invoice, August 1, 1822, Latimer Papers, Library of Congress; Michael Greenberg, *British Trade and the Opening of China, 1800–1842* (Cambridge: Cambridge University Press, 1951), pp. 153–58.

17. Letter: Richard Dale to John Barry, March 20, 1788, Miscellaneous Manuscript Collection, NYHS; Watson, *Annals,* II, pp. 337–39; Duvall, "Commerce," p. 413; Latourette, *Relations,* p. 69. Pacific relics gathered on this voyage were given to Charles Peale for his museum.

18. Samuel Woodhouse, "Log and Journal of the Ship 'United States' on a Voyage to China in 1784," *PMHB* 55, no. 3 (1931), 225–58.

19. Letters: Thomas Truxtun to Clement Biddle, December 6, 1787, June 24, 1789, Truxtun-Biddle Letters, LC; Benjamin Fuller to Thomas Truxtun, December 31, 1785, Society Miscellaneous Collection, HSP; "Memorandum of Mr. Hazard of the Sailing Ship Canton," n.d., Donnaldson Papers.

20. The unusual quality of these ships was noted by the *Asia*'s captain, who described the *Rousseau* as the only ship that could match the *Asia*'s speed. When the *Voltaire* sailed into Antwerp in 1802, it was a subject of great public curiosity. Girard received a letter describing the vessel as "the largest ship that has been in the Scheld for fifty years." Letters: Joseph Curwen to SG, May 7, 1802; John Girard to SG, May 4, 1784; SG to John Ferrers, March 12, 1795; John Ferrers to SG, April 13, 1795; Harold Gillingham, *Marine Insurance in Philadelphia 1721–1800* (Philadelphia: privately printed, 1933), p. 85; James Hedges, *The Browns of Providence Plantation,* II (Providence, R.I.: Brown University Press, 1968), p. 99; Jonathan Goldstein, "The Ethics of Tribute Versus the Profits of Trade: Stephen Girard's China Trade, 1787–1824," unpublished Senior Honors Thesis, University of Pennsylvania, 1969, p. 49; Clark, *Barry,* 329–49.

21. Mathew Carey, *The New Olive Branch* (Philadelphia: M. Carey & Sons, 1821), p. 113.

22. Frank Taussig, *The Tariff History of the United States* (New York: Putnam, 1910), p. 15; Albert Giesecke, *American Commercial Policy Before 1789* (New York: Appleton, 1910), p. 138; Emory Johnson et al., *History of the Domestic and Foreign Commerce of the United States* (Washington, D.C.: Carnegie Institution of Washington, 1915), p. 338; Klopfer, "Statistics," p. 221; Duvall, "Commerce," pp. 133–34; Latourette, *Relations,* p. 78.

23. United States, Congress, House, *Statement exhibiting the Value of Imports from China annually from 1821 to 1839,* H. Doc. 248, 26th Cong., 1st. sess., 1840, pp. 22–27.

24. Osmond Tiffany, *The Canton Chinese* (Boston and Cambridge: James Munroe, 1849), p. 73.

25. Will of Martha Washington of Mount Vernon, September 22, 1800, Fairfax County Courthouse, Fairfax, Va., noted Van Braam's gift to her of "a set of tea China, every piece having M. W. on it." See also (Carson), "Hollingsworth Book," bound volume of clippings and manuscript owned by Dr. and Mrs. John Carson, Newton Square, Pa.; *University Hospital Antiques Show/1972* (catalog), pp. 159–77; Edith Gates, "The Washington China," *The Quotarian* 10, no. 2 (1932), 5–6; Edward Barnsley, *History of China's Retreat* (Bristol, Pa.: Bristol Printing Co., 1933), p. 7; Joseph Downs, "A Chinese Lowestoft Toddy Jar," *Bulletin of the Metropolitan Museum of Art* 30, no. 2 (1935), 39–40; John Sweeney, *The Treasure House of Early American*

Rooms (New York: Viking, 1963), p. 69; Jean Mudge, *Chinese Export Porcelain for the American Trade. 1785–1835* (Newark: University of Delaware Press, 1962); "Colonial Homes," *Every Evening;* Loehr, "Van Braam," p. 182.

26. Henry Ingram, *The Life and Character of Stephen Girard* (Philadelphia: E. Stanley Hart, 1884), p. 124; *INA; The China Trade and Its Influences* (New York: Metropolitan Museum of Art, 1941), pp. 14–17; Margaret Jourdain and R. Soame Jenyns, *Chinese Export Art in the Eighteenth Century* (London: Spring Books, 1967), p. 36; Carl Crossman, *The China Trade* (Princeton: Pyne Press, 1972), pp. 53–54, 82; *University Hospital Antiques,* pp. 158–59.

27. Some confusion has existed concerning the provenance of the forgeries. Mason, Fielding, and Keyes have considered the Philadelphia merchant James Henry Blight (1796–1880) as the individual who had the copies made in Canton. This is clearly impossible, as Blight was only six years old in 1802 when Stuart took out his injunction against their sale. Blight did bring a Stuart "Washington" with him when he returned to Philadelphia from Canton in 1835, but that was a Stuart original which had hung in the Canton home of his relative James Oliver. It may have been from this original that Sword's copies were taken; but Blight could hardly have been a party to that act. George Mason, *The Life and Works of Gilbert Stuart* (New York: Scribner, 1879), pp. 114–15; Mantle Fielding, *Gilbert Stuart's Portraits of George Washington* (Philadelphia: Printed for the Subscribers, 1923), p. 171; Homer Keyes, "A Chinese Washington," *Antiques* 15, no. 2 (1929), 111; "Portrait of Washington," *PMHB* 26 (1902), 288. For correct account, see *Stuart* v. *Sword,* United States District Court for the Eastern District of Pennsylvania, Equity Dockets, vol. I, p. 88; Stuart petition, May 14, 1802; injunction, May 26, 1802, all in HSP; Elizabeth Johnston, *Original Portraits of Washington* (Boston: James R. Osgood, 1882), pp. 96–106; E. P. Richardson, "China Trade Portraits of Washington After Stuart," *PMHB* 94, no. 1 (1970), 95–100.

28. John to Henry Latimer, December 6, 1833, John R. Latimer Papers, University of Delaware Library, Newark; Rodris Roth, *Floor Coverings in 18th-Century America* (Washington, D.C.: Smithsonian Institution Press, 1967), p. 27; *China Trade,* p. 16; Sweeney, *Treasure House,* p. 69; *University Hospital Antiques,* cover and pp. 163–66.

29. Thomas Morton and Frank Woodbury, *History of the Pennsylvania Hospital* (Philadelphia: Times Printing House, 1895), pp. 322–26; Francis Packard, *Some Account of the Pennsylvania Hospital* (Philadelphia: Engle Press, 1938), pp. 93–95.

30. H. A. Crosby Forbes, "American Vision," pp. 53–54.

31. *Guide to the Philadelphia Museum* (Philadelphia: From the Museum Press, 1816), p. 7; Earl Bond, *Dr. Kirkbride and His Mental Hospital* (Philadelphia: Lippincott, 1947), p. 61; Joseph Jackson, *Encyclopedia of Philadelphia,* IV (Harrisburg: National Historical Association, 1933), pp. 1157–58; Davis, *History,* p. 133; Green, *History,* p. 108.

32. Letter: SG to Baring Brothers, January 18, 1808. Agreement with Isaac White, Builder, 1804; Agreement between Stephen Girard and Isaac White for Building, 25 July 1805; Articles of Agreement with Joseph Grice, 1808. See also Letters: SG to William Thomas & Son, December 22, 1804; to Baring Brothers, January 18, 1808; William Kirschbaum, "Famous Old Ship," *The New Bedford Standard,* ca. 1905; Brewington, "Philadelphia," p. 109.

33. On Girard ships, see also Letters: SG to William Thomas & Son (New York) December 22, 1804; to Baring Brothers (London), January 18, 1808; Jno Sullivan to SG, October 19, 1826. Pennsylvania *Official Documents* (1891), Bureau of Industrial Statistics, No. 10, "Commerce, Navigation and Ship-Building on the Delaware," IV (Harrisburg, 1897), p. 13; Stephen Simpson, *Biography of Stephen Girard* (Philadelphia: Thomas C. Bonsal, 1832), pp. 43–199; Abraham Ritter, *Philadelphia and Her Merchants* (Philadelphia: by the author, 1860), p. 74; W. S. Lindsay, *History of Merchant Shipping and Ancient Commerce*, III (London: Sampson Low, Marston, Low, and Searle, 1876), p. 8; Webster Christman, "The Papers of Stephen Girard," *Proceedings of the American Philosophical Society* 110 (1966), 385; Michael Costagliola, "The Canton Packet Cohota," *American Neptune* 7 (1947), 5; Charles Paullin, *Diplomatic Negotiations of American Naval Officers* (Baltimore: Johns Hopkins Press, 1912), p. 165; Winslow, *Biographies,* pp. 181–85; Brewington, "Philadelphia," pp. 109–10.

34. Letter: Thomas Truxtun to David Lewis, December 19, 1818, Miscellaneous Manuscript Collection, NYHS. Gillingham, *Insurance,* p. 100; Gares, "Girard," p. 208; John McMaster, *The Life and Times of Stephen Girard,* I (Philadelphia: Lippincott, 1918), pp. 303–4; Stephen Simpson, *Girard,* p. 95; Winslow, *Biographies,* pp. 181–85; Thill, "Delawarean," pp. 262–63; *Desilver's Philadelphia Directory* (Philadelphia, 1830), p. 9; *M'Elroy's Philadelphia Directory* (Philadelphia: Orrin Rogers, 1841), p. 12; 1842 ed., pp. 12, 326.

35. Joseph Leach, *The History of the Girard National Bank of Philadelphia* (Philadelphia: Lippincott, 1902), pp. 16–25.

36. Letter: SG to C. Evans, February 11, 1823, July 28, 1825. *The Register of Pennsylvania* (Philadelphia) 3, no. 9 (1829), 133–34; W. Frank Gorrecht, "Stephen Girard's Connection with Lancaster County," *Historical Papers and Addresses of the Lancaster County Historical Society* 29 (1955), 123–24; Jules Bogen, *The Anthracite Railroads* (New York: Ronald Press, 1927), pp. 14–15; Stephen Simpson, *Girard,* p. 197.

37. Henry Simpson, *The Lives of Eminent Philadelphians Now Deceased* (Philadelphia: William Brotherhead, 1859), p. 929; Charles Morris, *Makers of Philadelphia* (Philadelphia: L. R. Hamersly, 1894), p. 249; Carol Ranshaw, "Calendar of the University of Delaware John R. Latimer China Trade Papers," unpublished master's thesis, School of Library Science, Drexel Institute of Technology, 1953, pp. ii–20; Forrest MacDonald, *We the People* (Chicago: University of Chicago Press, 1958), p. 60; J. Thomas Scharf and Thompson Westcott, *History of Philadelphia 1609–1884,* III (Philadelphia: L. H. Everts, 1884), p. 2213; Charles Hummel, "John Latimer," pp. 269–73; Winslow, *Biographies,* pp. 129–32; Livingood, *Rivalry,* p. 91.

38. The voyage of the *Caledonia* from Philadelphia to Canton in 1819 was financed in part through a $23,270 loan from the New York Insurance Co. Robert Waln, Sr., 1815–1819 Letterbook, entry of April 19, 1819, WP, LC, on deposit with HSP.

39. William Hinshaw, *Encyclopedia of American Quaker Genealogy,* 2 vols. (Ann Arbor: Edwards Brothers, 1938); John Jordan, ed., *Colonial Families of Philadelphia,* 2 vols. (New York: Lewis, 1911); Thill, "Delawarean," pp. 293–94; Goldstein, "China Trade," pp. 25–27.

40. For records of Philadelphia China trade maritime insurance, see the "Marine Blotter" and other documents in the Archives and Historical Collection of the Insurance Company of North America, Philadelphia. A list of

"Substantial Participants in Philadelphia's China Trade, 1682–1846 (Shippers, Investors, Consignees)" and of "Duration of Residence of Philadelphians in China, 1784–1849" appear in Goldstein, "China Trade," pp. 29–32, drawn chiefly from lists published in *The Chinese Repository* (Canton, 1832–51) and *An Anglochinese Calendar for the Year 1844* (Macao: Printed at the Office of the *Chinese Repository,* 1844).

41. William Cornell, *The History of Pennsylvania* (Philadelphia: John Sully, 1876), pp. 414, 506–7; Gustavus Myers, *History of the Great American Fortunes* (New York: Modern Library, 1937), p. 79; Scharf and Westcott, *History,* II, p. 1226; Jackson, *Encyclopedia,* IV, pp. 1157–58.

42. Jacques Downs, "Fair Game: Exploitive Role-Myths and the American Opium Trade," *PHR* 41, no. 2 (May 1972), 133–49.

43. Thomas Fitzsimons of Pennsylvania, before House of Representatives, 1st Cong., 1st sess., April 14, 1789, in Joseph Gales, *The Debates and Proceedings in the Congress of the United States,* I (Washington, D.C.: Gales and Seaton, 1834), p. 141.

Chapter 4

1. Letter: SG to Mahlon Hutchinson and Myles McLeveen, January 2, 1806.

2. The problem of glutting had been foreseen by Congressman Richard Henry Lee ten days after the return to New York of the *Empress of China.* He had written James Madison at that time that he feared that "our Countrymen will overdo this business—For now there appears everywhere a Rage for East India voyages, so that the variety of means may defeat the attainment of the end—A regulated & useful commerce with that part of the World." Letter: Richard Henry Lee to James Madison, May 30, 1785, in Lee, *Letters,* ed. Ballagh. On the problem of glutting, see also Timothy Pitkin, *A Statistical View of the Commerce of the United States* (New Haven: Durrie & Peck, 1835), p. 304; Letters: William A. Foster to Richard Ashurst, March 20, 1827, HSP, Unger Collection; Joseph Archer to Jabez Jenkins, November 10, 1833, HSP, Joseph Archer Letterbook, I; Nathan Dunn to Samuel Archer and I. C. Jones Oakford & Company, October 7, 1829, DL; Shaw, *Journals,* pp. 350–51; Speer, *Empire,* p. 62.

3. Letter: H. W. Boyd to Jonathan Meredith, October 23, 1798; Great Britain, Parliament, *Parliamentary Papers* (House of Lords), 1821, VII (June 30, 1820). "Minutes of Evidence Relative to the Trade with the East Indies and China," pp. 88–91; William Moulton, *A Concise Extract from the Sea Journal of William Moulton* (Utica: Printed for the author, 1804), p. 98; James Swan, *The Northwest Coast* (New York: Harper, 1857), pp. 423–24; Henry Ingram, *The Life of Jean Girard* (Philadelphia: Edition limited, 1888), pp. 1103–19; Wildes, *Midas,* pp. 210, 385.

4. "Statement of the Shipping Employed in the Trade to Canton," *The American Museum* 7 (March 1790), 128; Thomas Ruston, "Reply to the Above"; "Dr. Ruston's Answer," *The American Museum* 12 (August 1792), 91–92, 94. See also Samuel Shaw to John Jay, December 21, 1787, in Shaw, *Journals,* p. 353.

5. For a description of British trade, see Letter: Forester & Co. to SG,

November 22, 1822; David Owen, *British Opium Policy in China and India* (New Haven: Yale University Press, 1934).

6. Robert Bennet Forbes, *Personal Reminiscences* (Boston: Little, Brown, 1878), p. 174; Daniel Henderson, *Yankee Ships in China Seas* (New York: Hastings House, 1946), p. 161.

7. Letter: John Latimer to Henry Latimer, April 3, 1829. John R. Latimer Papers, University of Delaware Library, Newark.

8. Letter: Benjamin Wilcocks to John Latimer, April 26, 1829, Latimer Papers, Library of Congress.

9. Nathan Dunn and Co. employed Dunn, Jabez Jenkins, and Joseph Archer. Wetmore employed Samuel Rawle and James Legee, and Olyphant & Co., James Bancker. Letters: Joseph Archer to George Carter, February 3, 1834, Archer Letterbook, HSP; Nathan Dunn to Joseph Archer, February 2, 1830, DL; Peter Dobell, "Travels in Kamchatka and Siberia," *American Quarterly Review* 9 (March and June 1831), 53; William Hunter, *Bits of Old China* (London: Kegan Paul, Trench, 1885), p. 166; James Wetmore, *The Wetmore Family of America* (Albany: Munsell & Rowland, 1861), p. 358; *CR* 5 (January 1837), 413–15; 7 (April 1839), 637; 8 (June 1839), 76.

10. W[illiam] Wood, *Sketches of China: With Illustrations From Original Drawings* (Philadelphia: Carey and Lea, 1830), pp. 206–7; Enoch Wines, *A Peep at China, in Mr. Dunn's Chinese Collection* (Philadelphia: Printed for Nathan Dunn, 1839), pp. 10–11; Dobell, "Travels," p. 53.

11. Letter: John Latimer to Joseph Lesley, June 23, 1847, Latimer Papers, University of Delaware; Ranshaw, "Calendar," p. 23.

12. Mathew Carey, "Essays on the Public Charities of Philadelphia," in *Miscellaneous Essays* (Philadelphia: Carey & Hurt, 1830), p. 173.

13. Dobell, "Travels," p. 53.

14. For the Chinese legal viewpoint, see Immanuel Hsu, *China's Entrance into the Family of Nations* (Cambridge: Harvard University Press, 1968), pp. 6–7.

15. Letter: SG to Mahlon Hutchinson, January 2, 1806.

16. Charles Stelle, "American Trade in Opium to China Prior to 1820," *PHR* 9 (December 1940), 429; Gertrude Kimball, *The East-India Trade of Providence from 1787 to 1807* (Providence: Preston and Rounds, 1896), p. 17.

17. United States Congress, Senate, *Message of the President (on) Commerce and Navigation in the Turkish Dominions,* S. Doc. 200, 25th Cong., 3d sess., 1839, pp. 81–86; Jacques Downs, "American Merchants and the China Opium Trade, 1800–1840," *Business History Review* 42 (Winter 1968), 421; Stelle, "Trade," 430–41. See also Letter: SG to Mahlon Hutchinson and Myles McLeveen, January 2, 1806.

18. Letters: Woodmas and Offley to SG, September 27, 1815; Dutilh & Co. to SG, March 24, 1819; Benjamin Seebohm, *Memoirs of the Life and Gospel Labors of Stephen Grellet,* II (London: A. W. Bennett, 1860), p. 28; [John Stephens], *Incidents of Travel in Greece, Turkey, Russia and Poland,* I (New York: Harper, 1838), p. 189; David Finnie, *Pioneers East* (Cambridge: Harvard University Press, 1967), p. 29; Walter Wright, "American Relations with Turkey to 1831," unpublished Ph.D. dissertation, Princeton University, 1928, p. 67.

19. Hosea Morse, *The International Relations of the Chinese Empire,* I (London: Longmans, Green, 1910), pp. 201–11; Morse, "The Provision of Funds for the East India Company's Trade," *Journal of the Royal Asiatic Society,* Part

II (April 1922), p. 227; Letters, George Blight to SG, March 4, November 21, 1807; Charles Macfarlane, *Constantinople in 1828* (London: Saunders and Otley, 1829), p. 33; Wright, "Relations," p. 53; Stelle, "American Opium Trade to China Prior to 1820," *PHR* 9 (December, 1940), 432–33.

20. Letter: John Latimer to Mary Latimer, March 28, 1831, Latimer Papers, Library of Congress.

21. On opposition to the British East India Company monopoly by Latimer and others, see Letter: An American Merchant [John Latimer], *The National Gazette*, October 27, 1828; Paul Pickowicz, "William Wood in Canton," *EIHC* 107 (January 1971), 3–24; *CR* 6 (May 1837), 44–47; *CR* 11 (January 1842), 1–2. See also Letter: John Latimer to Henry Latimer, April 4, 1833, John R. Latimer Papers, University of Delaware Library. Hunter, *Bits,* p. 276.

22. W. C. Hunter, *The Fan Kwae in Canton Before the Treaty Days* (London: Kegan Paul, 1882), pp. 101–13; Frank King and Prescott Clark, *A Research Guide to China-Coast Newspapers* (Cambridge: East Asian Research Center, Harvard University, 1965), pp. 15–131; Benjamin Silliman, *Mr. Dunn's Chinese Collection in Philadelphia* (Philadelphia: Brown, Bicking & Guilbert, 1841), pp. 14–15; Wood, *Sketches;* Latourette, *Relations,* pp. 82–180.

23. Letter: John Latimer to Sarah Latimer, April 28, 1827, Latimer Papers, University of Delaware. Peter Parker, "Thirteenth Annual Report of the Opthalmic Hospital at Canton," *CR* 14 (October 1845), 450; *Friend of China and Hong Kong Gazette* (Victoria) 3 (August 7, 1844), 459; (August 28, 1844), 483; *CR* 14 (January 1845), 5; 16 (January 1847), 5; (July 1847), 346; Simpson, *Lives,* p. 618; Morris, *Makers,* p. 99; Thill, "Delawarean," pp. 151, 268.

24. Elisha Kane, fragment of a diary or letter, January 24, 1845, Whampoa Medical Affairs, Elisha Kane Papers, APSL.

25. Letters: SG to Robert Smith, January 1, 1810; to C. J. Burke, May 18, 1814; to Myles McLeveen and Edward George, April 8, 1818; George Biddle Papers, *passim,* 1805–12, Cadwalader Collection; HSP; Wildes, *Midas,* pp. 166–67.

26. David Porter, *Journal of a Cruise Made to the Pacific Ocean,* II (New York: Wiley & Halstead, 1822), pp. 78–83, 144–78; George Preble, *The First Cruise of the United States Frigate Essex* (Salem: The Essex Institute, 1870), p. 73; Lindsay, *Shipping,* III, p. 8; Scharf and Westcott, *History,* I, p. 564; White, "Trade," pp. 17–18.

27. Letters: John Latimer to William Waln, October 19, 1815, Joseph Downs Memorial Manuscript Collection, Winterthur Museum, Greenville, Del.; Consequa to Peter Dobell, April 3, 1813, Miscellaneous Manuscript Collection, LC; C. J. Ingersol to Benjamin Wilcocks, May 14, 1822, Society Miscellaneous Collection HSP. Te-kong Tong, *United States Diplomacy in China, 1844–60* (Seattle: University of Washington Press, 1964), pp. 13–16; Thill, "Delawarean," p. 74.

28. Letter: John Latimer to Henry Latimer, April 3, 1829, Latimer Papers, University of Delaware. For other accounts of the bribery procedure, see Letter: H. Lockwood, August 12, 1838, *FMC* 7, no. 5 (May 1839), 142; and Wood, *Sketches,* pp. 206–17.

29. United States Congress, House, *Memorial of Russell Sturgis, et al., Canton, May 25, 1839,* H. Doc. 40, 26th Cong., 1st sess., 1840; Ranshaw,

"Latimer Papers," pp. ii–20; Morse, *Gilds,* p. 79. See also typed copy of a manuscript by Captain James W. Goodrich, NYHS, Goodrich Papers.

30. Letters: John Latimer to Benjamin Wilcocks, December 6, 1829, Latimer Papers, Library of Congress; Samuel Russell to E. C. Jenckes, December 17, 1821, Nightingale-Jenks Papers, Rhode Island Historical Society, Providence; Greenberg, *British Trade,* pp. 56–57; Latourette, *Relations,* p. 20; Morse, *Chronicles,* III, pp. 318–20; Downs, "Merchants," p. 441.

31. Letter: Charles King to Talbot, Olyphant & Co., ca. 1837–38. Charles Talbot Papers, property of Miss Frances Talbot, on deposit with APSL; White, "Hong," pp. 128–49.

32. Cheong, "Trade," pp. 45–46.

33. Morse, *Chronicles,* III, p. 237; Downs, "Merchants," p. 425.

34. Letters: Samuel Wagner to SG, October 28, 1815; Arthur Greland to SG, October 29, 1815; John Latimer to William Waln, October 29, 1815, Winterthur Museum, Downs Collection, Latimer Letterbook, 1815–16.

35. United States Congress, House, *Message of President Van Buren Transmitting a Report of the Secretary of State,* H. Doc. 71, 26th Cong., 2d sess., 1841; Morse, *Chronicles,* III, 318–20; Downs, "Merchants," pp. 425–26; Dennett, *Americans,* pp. 119–21.

36. The figure for 1821–22 is average of conflicting estimates given in Morse, *International Relations,* I, pp. 210–11; Greenberg, *British Trade,* p. 220; John Phipps, *A Practical Treatise on the Chinese and Eastern Trade* (Calcutta: Printed at the Baptist Mission Press, 1835), p. 313.

37. Most official American correspondence relating to the event was reproduced in United States Congress, House, *Message of President Van Buren,* H. Doc. 71, 26th Cong., 2d sess., 1841. Other accounts include *CR* 2 (January 1834), 423; Letters: Edward George to SG, October 1, November 16, 1821; Edwin Jenckes to Samuel Nightingale, October 21, 1821, Nightingale-Jenks Papers; "Execution of an American at Canton," *North American Review* 40 (January 1831), 58–68; S. Wells Williams, *The Middle Kingdom,* II (New York: Marlin Co., 1883), 461.

38. "Opium Trade With China," *Niles' Weekly Register* 23, no. 16 (December 21, 1822), 249–50.

39. Letter: Edward George to SG, November 16, 1821.

40. Letter: William Peter Van Veen & Sons to SG, December 17, 1822.

41. Kenneth Porter, *John Jacob Astor. Business Man,* II (Cambridge: Harvard University Press, 1931), pp. 613–14, 666; Downs, "Merchants," p. 430; Dennett, *Americans,* p. 118.

42. Randall to Alexander Hamilton, August 14, 1791, in *Hamilton,* ed. Cole.

43. Earl Cranston, "The Rise and Decline of Occidental Intervention in China," *PHR* 12 (March 1943), 23–24; Paullin, *Diplomatic Negotiations,* p. 182. Letter: John Latimer to Henry Latimer, September 30, 1821, Latimer Papers, University of Delaware.

44. Letter: John Latimer to Henry Latimer, November 1829, Latimer Papers, University of Delaware.

45. T. S. Tsiang, "The Extension of Equal Commercial Privileges to Other Nations After the Treaty of Nanking," *Chinese Social and Political Science Review* 15 (October 1931), 435; Hosea Morse and Harley MacNair, *Far Eastern International Relations* (Boston: Houghton Mifflin, 1931), p. 134.

46. Diplomatic theory held that the "consul . . . is not invested with any

diplomatic powers, and therefore is not entitled to communicate with the Government of the country in which he resides." United States Congress, Senate, *General Instructions to the Consuls and Commercial Agents of the United States,* S. Doc. 83, 22d Cong., 2d sess., p. 13; United States Congress, *Message of President Van Buren;* Robert Waln, Jr., "Embassy From the United States to China," *National Gazette,* February 5, 7, 20, 21, 1821; From a correspondent, "Outline of a Consular Establishment," *CR* 6 (May 1837), 69–82; Letter: John Latimer to Sarah Latimer, April 28, 1827, Latimer Papers, University of Delaware.

47. Forbes, *Personal Reminiscences,* p. 150; Downs, "American Merchants," p. 435; Morse, *International Relations,* I, p. 210. Averages taken from slightly different figures in Greenberg, *British Trade,* p. 220, come out virtually the same.

48. Paullin, *Negotiations,* pp. 183–84.

49. For eyewitness accounts and Chinese and American documents on the immediate antecedents of the Opium War, see *CR* 7 (March and April 1839), 599–656; 8 (May 1839), 1–37, 57–83; Fitch Taylor, *The Flag Ship,* II (New York: Appleton, 1840), pp. 110–11.

50. United States House, *Memorial of Sturgis;* Letter: King to Talbot, ca. 1837–38. See also Letter: William Waln to Lewis Waln, August 12, 1840, Society Miscellaneous Collection, HSP.

51. United States House, *Memorial of Sturgis.*

52. United States Congress, Senate, *Correspondence Between the Commander of the East India Squadron and Foreign Powers . . . During the Years 1842 and 1843,* S. Doc. 139, 29th Cong., 1st sess., pp. 21–36; *CR* 12, no. 8 (1843), 443–44; Dennett, *Americans,* p. 124; Tong, *Diplomacy,* pp. 13–16; see also the series of letters between Kearny and the members of Olyphant & Co. in the Charles Nicoll Talbot Papers owned by Frances Talbot.

53. White, "Trade," p. 44.

54. "Exports to Foreign Countries from the Port of Philadelphia," *Philadelphia Price Current* 1 (February 16, 1828), 155; Robert Waln, Jr., "Abstract of Philadelphia Trade to Canton," WP; Dennett, *Americans,* p. 10.

55. Letters: James Bancker to C. N. Bancker, August 24, 1842, October 26, 1846; to Anne Bancker, January 17, 1846, JB; John Dorsey Sword, Business Letters, *passim,* HSP. Thill, "Delawarean," pp. 114, 262–63.

56. W. Cameron Forbes, "Houqua: the Merchant Prince of China. 1769–1843," *Bulletin of the American Asiatic Association* 6 (December 1940), 9–18; William Cadbury and Mary Jones, *At the Point of a Lancet: One Hundred Years of the Canton Hospital, 1835–1935* (Shanghai: Kelly and Walsh, Limited, 1935); Kwang-Ching Liu, *Anglo-American Steamship Rivalry in China* (Cambridge: Harvard University Press, 1962), pp. 12, 16, 179; Downs, "Merchants," p. 426.

57. George Cooke, *China* (London: G. Routledge, 1858), p. 179.

58. United States Congress, Senate, *Dispatches from . . . Ministers to China,* Letter, William Reed to Secretary of State Cass, June 30, 1858, S. Ex. Doc. 30, 36th Cong., 1st sess., p. 357. See also John Fairbank, "The Legalization of the Opium Trade Before the Treaties of 1858," *Chinese Social and Political Science Review* 17 (July 1933), 215–63; Owen, *British Opium,* p. 265.

59. Shaw, *Journals,* p. 133.

60. Letter: Arthur Grelaud to SG, May 16, 1816; Nora Waln, *The House of Exile* (Boston: Little, Brown, 1933), pp. 3–17; Wildes, *Midas,* p. 269;

Girard College artifacts are catalogued A-2, 2046, R-2046, and #50; *China Trade*, p. 17, figure 92.

61. Hunter, *Fan Kwae*, pp. 40, 48.

62. W. Cameron Forbes, "Houqua," pp. 9–14. See also: John Murray Forbes, *Reminiscences of John Murray Forbes*, ed. Sarah Hughes, I (Boston: George H. Ellis, 1902), pp. 140–41; Robert Bennet Forbes, *Reminiscences*, 3rd ed. rev., 1892, pp. 370–71.

63. Benjamin Low, "Houqua," in *The China Trade Post-Bag of the Seth Low Family*, ed. Elma Loines (Manchester, Me.: Falmouth Publishing House, 1953), p. 60. See also the following commentary by American traders on the uprightness of Chinese merchants: "Generosity and Gratitude of a Chinese Merchant," in Freeman Hunt, ed., *Worth and Wealth: A Collection of Maxims, Morals, and Miscellanies for Merchants and Men of Business* (New York: Stringer & Townsend, 1856), p. 82; a similar account appears on p. 110.

Chapter 5

1. Letters: James Bancker to his sister, April 6, 1843; to his mother, June 20, 1843. JB.

2. Proclus, "On the Genius of the Chinese," *Port Folio* 5 (April 1811), 343–56; (May 1811), 418–32; 6 (August 1811), 115–20, 133; Miller, "Chinese Image," p. 195; Stanton, *Spots*, pp. 19–22.

3. "For the Port Folio—On China," *Port Folio*, 4th series, 7 (February 1819), 91–111.

4. Thomson, entry, January 1, 1768, First Minute Book; Thomson, "Preface," *TAPS* 1 (January 1769–January 1771), iii–xviii. On the general theoretical orientation which underlay APS interest in China, in the post-Revolutionary period, see Whitfield Bell, Jr., "The Scientific Environment of Philadelphia, 1775–1790," *Proceedings of the American Philosophical Society* 92 (March 1948), 6–14.

5. Humphry Marshall, *Arbustrum Americanum* (Philadelphia: J. Crukshank, 1785), p. vi.

6. *Guide to the Philadelphia Museum*, p. 6; Davis, *History*, p. 133; Green, *History*, p. 108; Jackson, *Encyclopedia*, IV, pp. 1157–58; Bond, *Dr. Kirkbride*, p. 61. See also Letters: Joseph Hopkinson, John Vaughan, Nathaniel Chapman to APS President, March 7, 1834; Peter Duponceau, Nathaniel Chapman, Joseph Hopkinson to Isaac Lea, Charles Meigs, A. D. Bache, November 18, 1835, Miscellaneous Manuscript Collection, APSL; Peter Duponceau to John Bailey, April 16, 22, 1830, Washburn Papers, MHS; Conklin, "American Philosophical," p. 238.

7. Clay Lancaster, "The Chinese Influence in American Architecture and Landscaping," in *Nineteenth Annual Washington Antiques Show/1974* (catalogue), p. 36; H. A. Crosby Forbes, "American Vision," p. 51.

8. William Birch, *The Country Seats of the United States* (Springfield, Pa.: W. Birch, 1808), #19; William Birch, "Autobiography," MS in HSP; Andreas van Braam Houckgeest, *Voyage de l'Ambassade de la Compagnie des Indes Orientales*, I (Philadelphie: M. L. E. Moreau de Saint-Méry, 1797), pp. iii–xvi; Ruth Seltzer, "The Best of Two Old River Houses," *Evening Bulletin* (Philadelphia), December 10, 1957, p. 58; Marion Rivinus and Katharine

Biddle, *Lights Along the Delaware* (Philadelphia: Dorrance, 1965), p. 71; Barnsley, *History*, pp. 4–9. A watercolor painting of "China Retreat" by Birch is in the Library Company.

9. Harold Eberlein and Cortlandt Hubbard, *Portrait of a Colonial City. Philadelphia: 1670–1838* (Philadelphia: Lippincott, 1939), p. 478. The first group of Chinese immigrants also came to Philadelphia, in 1785. La Fargue, "Chinese," pp. 129–30.

10. William Birch, Autobiography, Society Miscellaneous Collection, HSP; Janet Thorpe, "Chinoiserie in America with Emphasis on the Van Braam Houckgeest Collection," term paper, Institute of Fine Arts, New York University, May 1964, pp. 14–16; M[argaret] Jourdain, "The China Trade and Its Influence on Works of Art," *Apollo* 34 (November 1941), 111; Davis, *History of Bucks County*, p. 133; La Fargue, "Chinese," pp. 130–31.

11. A. J. Downing, *A Treatise on the Theory and Practice of Landscape Gardening* (New York and London: Wiley and Putnam, 1841), p. 345; Lancaster, "Chinese," p. 92.

12. Lancaster, "Chinese," p. 93.

13. Thill, "Delawarean," pp. 221–22, 277. The china closet from "Latimeria" is also in the Winterthur Museum.

14. William Chambers, *Designs of Chinese Buildings* (London: Published for the author, 1757), Plate V; Oberholtzer, *Philadelphia*, II, p. 198; Lancaster, "Chinese," pp. 34, 93; H. A. Crosby Forbes, "American," p. 53.

15. Letters: Joseph Hopkinson, John Vaughan, Nathaniel Chapman to APS President, March 7, 1834; Peter Duponceau, Nathaniel Chapman, Joseph Hopkinson to Isaac Lea, Charles Meigs, A. D. Bache, November 18, 1835, Miscellaneous Manuscript Collection, APSL.

16. Wines, *Peep*, pp. vi–viii; H. A. Crosby Forbes, "American Vision," pp. 52–53.

17. Wines, *Peep*, pp. vi–viii. Wines' volume was included in *Sermons Collected by the American Sunday School Union*, 3, no. 27 (n.d.) under the title: "A Descriptive Catalogue of the Chinese Collection in Philadelphia."

18. [Benjamin Silliman], "Nathan Dunn's Chinese Collection at Philadelphia," *American Journal of Science and Arts* 25, (January 1839), 391–92; Silliman, *Mr. Dunn's*, pp. 2–25; [Benjamin Silliman], "Chinese Museum," *Niles' National Register* (Washington) 55 (February 16, 1839), 391–92.

19. James Buckingham, *The Eastern and Western States of America*, II (London: Fisher, 1842), pp. 72–73. Additional praise was tendered to the museum by Jay Cooke, Brantz Meyer, George Combe, and Daniel Bowen. Daniel Bowen, *A History of Philadelphia* (Philadelphia: Daniel Bowen, 1839), pp. 85–86; Silliman, *Mr. Dunn's*, pp. 2–25; Oberholtzer, *Philadelphia*, II, p. 199.

20. Elijah Bridgman, "A Peep at China," *CR* 8, no. 11 (March 1840), 585.

21. Casper Souder, *The History of Chestnut Street* (Philadelphia: *Sunday Dispatch*, 1858), pp. 148–49; Henry Shinn, *History of Mount Holly* (Mt. Holly, N.J.: privately printed, 1957), p. 157; Hummel, "Dunn," p. 39. See also John Peters, *Miscellaneous Remarks upon the Chinese* (Philadelphia: G. B. Zieber, 1847); H. A. Crosby Forbes, "American Vision," p. 53.

22. Peter Duponceau and Charles Gutzlaff, *Two Letters on the Chinese System of Writing* (Philadelphia: Printed by William S. Young, 1840); Duponceau, *A Dissertation on the . . . Chinese System of Writing* (Philadelphia: Pub-

lished for the American Philosophical Society, 1838); Duponceau, "On . . . the Nature of the Chinese Language," *Philosophical Magazine* (London) 5 (January 1829), 15–24.

23. Clifton Phillips, *Protestant America and the Pagan World* (Cambridge: Harvard University Press, 1969), p. 173; Robert Waln, Jr., *China; Comprehending a View of the Origin . . . of That Empire* (Philadelphia: J. Maxwell, 1823), pp. v, 473.

24. Robert Waln, Jr., "Infanticide in China," *National Gazette* (Philadelphia), January 15, 16, 17, 182.

25. *Early Proceedings of the American Philosophical Society From 1744–1838* (Philadelphia: Press of McCalla & Stavely, 1884), p. 246; Braam, *Voyage de l'Ambassade*, I, pp. iii–iv.

26. Conroy and Miyakawa, *East*, p. xi.

27. Luther Spoehr, "Sambo and the Heathen Chinee: Californians' Racial Stereotypes in the Late 1870's," *PHR* 42 (May 1973), 191; Robert Heizer and Alan Almquist, *The Other Californians: Prejudice and Discrimination under Spain, Mexico, and the United States to 1920* (Berkeley: University of California Press, 1970), p. 197; Alexander Saxton, *The Indispensable Enemy. Labor and the Anti-Chinese Movement in California* (Berkeley: University of California Press, 1971), pp. 268–72, 278.

28. Graham, "Ideas," Summary, n.p.

29. Letter: J. R. Latimer to Samuel Dupont, January 16, 1860. Eleutherian Mills Historical Library, Greenville, Del. Manuscript Collection.

China, by Robert Waln, Jr.

Bibliography

Manuscript Sources

American Philosophical Society Library, Philadelphia. Elisha Kane Papers; First Minute Book, American Society; James Bancker Papers. Miscellaneous Manuscript Collection.

Carson, Dr. John. Newtown Square, Pennsylvania. "Hollingsworth Book" (MS).

Eleutherian Mills Historical Library, Greenville, Delaware. Manuscript Collection.

Estate of Stephen Girard, dec'd, Philadelphia. Stephen Girard Papers (on microfilm in American Philosophical Society Library, Philadelphia).

Fairfax County Courthouse, Fairfax, Virginia. Will of Martha Washington of Mount Vernon, September 22, 1800.

Historical Society of Montgomery County, Norristown, Pennsylvania. Donnaldson Papers.

Historical Society of Pennsylvania, Philadelphia. Joseph Archer Letterbook; Cadwalader Collection; Dreer Collection; Etting Papers; Kidd Letterbooks 1749–63; Society Miscellaneous Collection; Orr, Dunlope and Greenholme Letterbook; Pemberton Papers; Riché Letterbooks, 1750–71; Roberdeau Letterbook, 1764–71; John Dorsey Sword Business Letters; Unger Collection; Richard Waln, Jr., Mill Accounts; Waln Letterbook, 1766–99; Wharton Correspondence; Wharton Letterbook, 1752–59; Willing Letterbooks, 1754–61.

Insurance Company of North America, Philadelphia. Archives and Historical Collection.

Library Company of Philadelphia. Miscellaneous Manuscript Collection; Truxtun-Biddle Letters; Waln Family Papers. Library Company "Waln Papers" are almost entirely a post-Colonial collection not to be confused with "Richard Waln, Jr., Mill Accounts" and "Waln Letterbook, 1766–99," both owned by the Historical Society of Pennsylvania.

Library of Congress. Latimer Papers.

Mariner's Museum Library, Newport News, Virginia. Papers of Stewart, Nesbitt & Co.
Massachusetts Historical Society, Boston. Washburn Papers.
Mystic Seaport, Mystic, Connecticut. G. W. Blunt White Library Manuscript Collection. Nathan Dunn Letterbook, 1829–38.
New York Historical Society. Goodrich Papers; Miscellaneous Manuscript Collection.
New York Public Library. Constable-Pierrepont Collection, William Constable Shipping Papers.
Rhode Island Historical Society, Providence. Nightingale-Jenks Papers.
Talbot, Miss Frances. Charles Nicoll Talbot Papers (on deposit with American Philosophical Society Library, Philadelphia).
Thibault Family. Saint David's, Pennsylvania. John Green Papers.
University of Delaware Library, Newark. John R. Latimer Papers.
University of Pennsylvania Library Rare Book Collection, Philadelphia. "Receit Book, F. Molineux for Account of Captain Green," Canton, 1784 and 1786.
Winterthur Museum, Greenville, Delaware. Joseph Downs Memorial Manuscript Collection.

Published Contemporary Sources

United States Government Documents

Gales, Joseph. *The Debates and Proceedings in the Congress of the United States,* I. Washington, D.C.: Gales and Seaton, 1834.
U.S. Congress. Senate. *General Instructions to the Consuls and Commercial Agents of the United States.* S. Doc. 83, 22d Cong., 2d sess., 1833.
U.S. Congress. Senate. *Message of the President* [on] *Commerce and Navigation in the Turkish Dominions.* S. Doc. 200, 25th Cong., 3d sess., 1839.
U.S. Congress. House. *Memorial of Russell Sturgis, et al., Canton, May 25, 1839.* H. Doc. 40, 26th Cong., 1st sess., 1840.
U.S. Congress. House. *Statement Exhibiting the Value of Imports From China Annually From 1821 to 1839.* H. Doc. 248, 26th Cong., 1st sess., 1840.
U.S. Congress. House. *Message of President Van Buren Transmitting a Report of the Secretary of State.* H. Doc. 71, 26th Cong., 2d sess., 1841.
U.S. Congress. Senate. *Correspondence Between the Commander of the East India Squadron and Foreign Powers . . . During the Years 1842 and 1843.* S. Doc. 139, 29th Cong., 1st sess., 1844.
U.S. Congress. Senate. *Dispatches from . . . Ministers in China.* S. Ex. Doc. 30, 36th Cong., 1st sess., 1860.
Stuart vs. *Sword.* United States District Court for the Eastern District of Pennsylvania. Equity Dockets, vol. I, p. 88, 1802; Stuart Petition, May 14, 1802; Injunction, May 26, 1802; HSP.

Great Britain—Government Documents

Great Britain. Parliament. *Parliamentary Papers.* (House of Lords), 1821, vol. VII. "Minutes of Evidence Relative to the Trade with the East Indies and China."

Pennsylvania—Government Documents

Pennsylvania. *Official Documents* (1891). (Harrisburg, 1897).

Other Contemporary Publications

The American Apollo 1 (January 20, 1792), 21.
An American Merchant [John Latimer]. Letter. *National Gazette,* October 27, 1828.
An Anglochinese Calendar for the Year 1844. Macao: Printed at the Office of the *Chinese Repository,* 1844.
Anonymous note to Abel James and Henry Drinker, Fall 1773, in *PMHB* 15 (1891), 389–90.
Birch, William. *The Country Seats of the United States.* Springfield, Pa.: W. Birch, 1808.
Bowen, Daniel. *A History of Philadelphia.* Philadelphia: Daniel Bowen, 1839.
Braam Houckgeest, Andreas van. *Voyage de l'Ambassade de la Compagnie des Indes Orientales.* 2 vols. Philadelphie: M. L. E. Moreau de Saint-Méry, 1797–98.
Bridgman, Elijah. "A Peep at China." *Chinese Repository* 8, no. 11 (March 1840), 581–87.
Buckingham, James. *The Eastern and Western States of America.* London: Fisher, 1842.
By a Yankee. *The Adventures of a Yankee: or the Singular Life of John Ledyard.* Boston: Carter, Hendee and Babcock, 1831.
Carey, Mathew. "Essays on the Public Charities of Philadelphia," in *Miscellaneous Essays.* Philadelphia: Carey & Hart, 1830.
———. *The New Olive Branch.* Philadelphia: M. Carey & Sons, 1821.
Catesby, Mark. *Natural History of Carolina, Florida, and the Bahama Islands.* 2 vols. London: Printed at the expense of the author, 1743.
Chambers, William. *Designs of Chinese Buildings.* London: Published for the author, 1757.
The Chinese Repository. (Canton, 1832–51).
Cooke, George. *China.* London: G. Routledge, 1858.
Daily Advertiser (New York), May 16, 1785.
Delaware Gazette (Wilmington), January 18, 1786.
Desilver's Philadelphia Directory. Philadelphia, 1830.
Dobell, Peter. "Travels in Kamchatka and Siberia." *American Quarterly Review* 9 (March–June 1831), 52–81.
Downing, A. J. *A Treatise on the Theory and Practice of Landscape Gardening.* New York and London: Wiley and Putnam, 1841.
Du Halde, Jean. *A Description of China,* vol. 1. London: T. Gardner, 1738.
Duponceau, Peter. *A Dissertation on the . . . Chinese System of Writing.* Philadelphia: Published for the American Philosophical Society, 1838.
———. "On . . . the Nature of the Chinese Language." *Philosophical Magazine* (London) 5 (January 1829), 15–24.
———, and Charles Gutzlaff. *Two Letters on the Chinese System of Writing.* Philadelphia: Printed by William S. Young, 1840.
Early Proceedings of the American Philosophical Society From 1744–1838. Philadelphia: Press of McCalla & Stavely, 1884.

"Execution of an American at Canton." *North American Review* 40 (January 1831), 58–68.

"Exports to Foreign Countries from the Port of Philadelphia." *Philadelphia Price Current* 1 (February 16, 1828), 155.

Forbes, John Murray. *Reminiscences of John Murray Forbes.* 3 vols. Edited by Sarah Hughes. Boston: George H. Ellis, 1902.

Forbes, Robert Bennet. *Personal Reminiscences.* Boston: Little, Brown, and Company, 1878. 3rd. ed., rev., 1892.

"For the Port Folio—On China." *Port Folio.* 4th series, 7 (February 1819), 91–111.

Franklin, Benjamin. *The Autobiography of Benjamin Franklin.* Edited by Leonard Labaree, Ralph Ketcham, Helen Boatfield, and Helene Fineman. New Haven: Yale University Press, 1964.

———. *The Papers of Benjamin Franklin,* vol. VI. Edited by Leonard Labaree. New Haven: Yale University Press, 1963.

Freeman's Journal (Philadelphia), June 22, 1785.

Freneau, Philip. "On the First American Ship That Explored the Route to CHINA, and the EAST-INDIES, After the Revolution." *Poems Written Between the Years 1768 and 1794.* Monmouth, N.J.: At the Press of the Author, 1795.

The Friend of China and Hong Kong Gazette (Victoria) 3 (August 7, 1844), 459; (August 28, 1844), 483.

From a Correspondent. "Outline of a Consular Establishment." *CR* 6 (May 1837), 69–82.

Guide to the Philadelphia Museum. Philadelphia: "From the Museum Press," 1816.

Hamilton, Alexander. *The Industrial and Commercial Correspondence of Alexander Hamilton.* Edited by Arthur Cole. Chicago: A. W. Shaw, 1928.

Hunt, Freeman. *Lives of American Merchants,* vol. I. New York: Office of Hunt's Merchant's Magazine, 1856.

———, ed. *Worth and Wealth: A Collection of Maxims, Morals, and Miscellanies for Merchants and Men of Business.* New York: Stringer & Townsend, 1856.

Hunter, William. *Bits of Old China.* London: Kegan Paul, Trench, & Co., 1885.

———. *The Fan Kwae in Canton Before the Treaty Days.* London: Kegan Paul, Trench, & Co., 1882.

Jefferys, Thomas. *The Great Probability of a Northwest Passage.* London: Thomas Jefferys, 1768.

Jartoux, Pierre. "Lettre du Pere [sic] Jartoux . . . A Pekin, le 12. d'Avril 1711." *Lettres Edifiantes et Curieuses,* X (Paris: Jean Barbou, 1713), pp. 159–85.

Jay, John. *The Correspondence and Public Papers of John Jay,* vol. III. Edited by Henry Johnston. New York: G. P. Putnam, 1891.

Lafitau, Joseph. *Mémoire . . . Concernant . . . Gin-seng.* Montréal: Typographie de Senecal, 1858.

———. *Moeurs des Sauvages Amériquains,* vol. III. Paris: Saugrain and Hochereau, 1724.

Ledyard, John. *A Journal of Captain Cook's Last Voyage.* Hartford: Nathaniel Patten, 1783.

Lee, Richard Henry. *The Letters of Richard Henry Lee,* vol. II. Edited by James Ballagh. New York: Macmillan, 1914.

Loines, Elma, ed. *The China Trade Post-Bag of the Seth Low Family.* Manchester, Me.: Falmouth Publishing House, 1953.

Lockwood, H. Letter, August 12, 1838, *FMC* 7, no. 5 (May 1839), 142.

Macfarlane, Charles. *Constantinople in 1828.* London: Saunders and Otley, 1829.

MacPherson, David. *Annals of Commerce.* 3 vols. London: Nichols et al., 1805.

M'Elroy's Philadelphia Directory. Philadelphia: Orrin Rogers, 1841, 1842.

Marshall, Humphry. *Arbustrum Americanum.* Philadelphia: J. Crukshank, 1785.

Massachusetts Centinel (Boston), May 18, 1785.

Mattioli, Pier. *Commentarii in VI Libros De Medica Materia.* Venice: Apud Felicem Valgrisium, 1583.

Moulton, William. *A Concise Extract from the Sea Journal of William Moulton.* Utica, N.Y.: Printed for the Author, 1804.

Newport Mercury, May 21, 1785.

New York Packet, May 16, 1785.

North American Review 27 (October 1828), 562.

Nye, Gideon. "American Commerce with China." *The Far East* (Shanghai), new series 4 (January 1878), 14–21.

Parker, Peter. "Thirteenth Annual Report of the Opthalmic Hospital at Canton." *CR* 14 (October 1845), 449–64.

Pennsylvania Chronicle, March 7, 1768.

Pennsylvania Packet, January 3, 1774; May 16, 1785.

Peters, John R., Jr. *Miscellaneous Remarks upon the . . . Chinese.* Philadelphia: G. B. Zieber, 1847.

Phipps, John. *A Practical Treatise on the Chinese and Eastern Trade.* Calcutta: Printed at the Baptist Mission Press, 1835.

Pitkin, Timothy. *A Statistical View of the Commerce of the United States.* New Haven: Durrie & Peck, 1835.

Porter, David. *Journal of a Cruise Made to the Pacific Ocean.* 2 vols. New York: Wiley & Halstead, 1822.

"Portrait of Washington," *PMHB* 26, no. 2 (1902), 288.

Preble, George. *The First Cruise of the United States Frigate Essex.* Salem, Mass.: Essex Institute, 1870.

Proclus. "On the Genius of the Chinese." *Port Folio* 5 (April 1811), 342–56; (May 1811), 418–36; (June 1811), 493–506; 6 (Aug. 1811), 112–33.

Providence Gazette, May 18, 1785.

The Register of Pennsylvania (Philadelphia).

"Registers Granted at the Port of Philadelphia in the Quarter ending 5th January 1775," *PMHB* 39, no. 2 (1915), 93.

Reynolds, J[eremiah]. *Voyage of the United States Frigate Potomac.* New York: Harper & Brothers, 1835.

Ritter, Abraham. *Philadelphia and Her Merchants.* Philadelphia: Published by the author, 1860.

Robin, Claude. *Noveau Voyage dans l'Amérique 1781.* Philadelphia: Moutard, 1782.

Rush, Benjamin. "Observations [on] the Black Colour of the Negroes." *TAPS* 4 (1799), 289–97.

Ruston, Thomas. "Reply to the Above." *The American Museum* 12 (August 1792), 91–92. "Dr. Ruston's Answer," ibid., 94. Refers to Ruston-Swanwick debate in *The American Museum.*

Shaw, Samuel. *The Journals of Major Samuel Shaw, the First American Consul at Canton.* Edited by Josiah Quincy. Boston: Wm. Crosby and H. P. Nichols, 1847.

———. Letter to John Jay, May 19, 1785, in *American Museum* 1 (March 1787), 194–97.

———. "Remarks on the Commerce of America with China." *American Museum* 7 (March 1790), 126–28.

Silliman, Benjamin. "Chinese Museum." *Niles' National Register* (Washington) 55 (February 16, 1839), 391–92.

———. *Mr. Dunn's Chinese Collection in Philadelphia.* Philadelphia: Brown, Bicking & Guilbert, 1841.

———, M.D. "Nathan Dunn's Chinese Collection at Philadelphia." *American Journal of Science and Arts* 35 (January 1839), 391–400.

Simpson, Henry. *The Lives of Eminent Philadelphians Now Deceased.* Philadelphia: William Brotherhead, 1859.

Simpson, Stephen. *Biography of Stephen Girard.* Philadelphia: Thomas C. Bonsal, 1832.

Smith, Adam. *An Inquiry into the Nature and Causes of the Wealth of Nations.* 2 vols. London: Printed for W. Strahan, 1776.

Smith, William. "A Short Account of the Present State of the College." *The Universal Asylum and Columbian Magazine* 5 (1790), 274–76.

"Statement of the Shipping Employed in the Trade to Canton." *American Museum* 7 (March 1790), 128.

[Stephens, John.] *Incidents of Travel in Greece, Turkey, Russia and Poland.* 2 vols. New York: Harper & Brothers, 1838.

Swan, James. *The Northwest Coast.* New York: Harper & Brothers, 1857.

Swift, John White. Letter to John Swift, *PMHB* 9, no. 4 (1885), 485.

Taylor, Fitch. *The Flag Ship.* 2 vols. New York: Appleton, 1840.

[Thomson, Charles.] "Preface." *TAPS* 1 (January 1768–January 1771), i–xviii.

Thwaites, Reuben. *The Jesuit Relations and Allied Documents.* Cleveland: Burrows, 1896–1901, vols, LXVII, LXXI.

Tiffany, Osmond. *The Canton Chinese.* Boston and Cambridge: James Munroe, 1849.

Waln, Robert, Jr. *China; Comprehending a View of the Origin of that Empire & a Full Description of American Trade to Canton.* Philadelphia: J. Maxwell, 1823.

———. "Embassy from the United States to China." *National Gazette* (Philadelphia), February 5, 7, 20, 21, 1821.

———. "Infanticide in China." *National Gazette* (Philadelphia), January 15, 16, 17, 1821.

Watson, John. *Annals of Philadelphia and Pennsylvania.* 2 vols. Philadelphia: Carey & Hart, 1844.

Wharton, Samuel. "Observations on Consumption of Teas in North America." *PMHB* 25, no. 1 (1901), 139–41.

Williams, S. Wells. *The Middle Kingdom,* vol. 2. New York: Marlin, 1883.

Wines, Enoch. *A Peep at China, in Mr. Dunn's Chinese Collection.* Philadelphia: Printed for Nathan Dunn, 1839. Reprinted in *Sermons Collected by the American Sunday School Union* 3, no. 27 (n.d.).

Wood, W[illiams]. *Sketches of China: With Illustrations from Original Drawings.* Philadelphia: Carey and Lea, 1830.

Woodhouse, Samuel, ed. "Log and Journal of the Ship 'United States' on a Voyage to China in 1784." *PMHB* 55, no. 3 (1931), 225–58.

Secondary Materials

Allen, B. Sprague. *Tides in English Taste (1619–1800)*. New York: Pageant Books, 1958.

Augur, Helen. *Passage to Glory: John Ledyard's America*. Garden City, N.Y.: Doubleday, 1946.

Bailey, L. H., and Bailey, Ethel. *Hortus*. New York: Macmillan, 1935.

Balch, Edwin. "Arctic Expeditions Sent from the American Colonies." *PMHB* 31 (1907), 419–28.

Ball, J. Dyer. *Things Chinese*. London: Sampson Low, Marston and Company, 1900.

Barnsley, Edward. *History of China's Retreat*. Bristol, Pa.: Bristol Printing Company, 1933.

Bell, Whitfield, Jr. "The Scientific Environment of Philadelphia, 1775–1790." *Proceedings of the American Philosophical Society* 92 (March 1948), 6–14.

Bemis, Samuel. *A Diplomatic History of the United States*. New York: Henry Holt, 1951.

———. *Jay's Treaty*. New Haven: Yale University Press, 1962.

Biographical and Genealogical History of the State of Delaware. 2 vols. Chambersburg, Pa.: J. M. Runk, 1899.

Bogen, Jules. *The Anthracite Railroads*. New York: Ronald Press, 1927.

Bond, Earl. *Dr. Kirkbride and His Mental Hospital*. Philadelphia: Lippincott, 1947.

Brewington, Marion. "Maritime Philadelphia 1609–1837." *PMHB* 48 (April 1939), 93–117.

Bridenbaugh, Carl. *Cities in Revolt, Urban Life in America, 1743–1776*. New York: Knopf, 1955.

———, and Bridenbaugh, Jessica. *Rebels and Gentlemen. Philadelphia in the Age of Franklin*. London and New York: Oxford University Press, 1968.

Cadbury, William, and Jones, Mary. *At the Point of a Lancet: One Hundred Years of the Canton Hospital, 1835–1935*. Shanghai: Kelly and Walsh, 1935.

Campbell, John. *History of the Society of the Friendly Sons of Saint Patrick*. Philadelphia: Hibernian Society, 1892.

Channing, Edward. *History of the United States*. 3 vols. New York: Macmillan, 1916.

Cheong, W. E. "Trade and Finance in China, 1784–1834. A Reappraisal." *Business History* (Liverpool) 7, no. 1 (January 1965), 34–56.

China Trade and Its Influences, The. New York: Metropolitan Museum of Art, 1941.

Christman, Webster. "The Papers of Stephen Girard: Their Preparation and Historical Interest." *Proceedings of the American Philosophical Society* 110 (1966), 383–85.

Clark, William. *Gallant John Barry*. New York: Macmillan, 1938.

Cochran, Thomas C. *Basic History of American Business*, 2d ed. Princeton: Van Nostrand, 1968 [1950].

"Colonial Homes of Wilmington." *Every Evening* (Wilmington), December 13, 1913, p. 14.

The Compact Edition of the Oxford English Dictionary (1971).

Conklin, Edwin. "The American Philosophical Society and the Founders of Our government." *PH* 4, no. 4 (1937), 235–40.

Conroy, F. Hilary, and Miyakawa, T. Scott. *East Across the Pacific. Historical & Sociological Studies of Japanese Imigration & Assimilation.* Santa Barbara, Calif.: American Bibliographical Center Clio Press, 1972.

Coolidge, Mary. *Chinese Immigration.* New York: Henry Holt, 1919.

Corner, George. *Doctor Kane of the Arctic Seas.* Philadelphia: Temple University Press, 1972.

Costagliola, Michael. "The Canton Packet *Cohota.*" *American Neptune* 7 (1947), 5–7.

Cranston, Earl. "The Rise and Decline of Occidental Intervention in China." *PHR* 12 (March 1943), 23–32.

Crossman, Carl. *The China Trade.* Princeton: Pyne Press, 1972.

———. *An Exhibition and Sale of Paintings and Objects of the China Trade.* October 20–November 21, 1969 (brochure). Childs Gallery, Boston.

Cornell, William. *The History of Pennsylvania.* Philadelphia: John Sully, 1876.

Davis, William. *The History of Bucks County, Pennsylvania.* Doylestown, Pa.: Democrat Book and Job Office Print, 1876, p. 133.

Dennett, Tyler. *Americans in Eastern Asia.* New York: Macmillan, 1922.

Downs, Jacques. "American Merchants and the China Opium Trade, 1800–1840." *Business History Review* 42 (Winter 1968), 418–42.

———. "Fair Game: Exploitive Role-Myths and the American Opium Trade." *PHR* 41, no. 2 (May 1972) 133–49.

Downs, Joseph. "A Chinese Lowestoft Toddy Jar." *Bulletin of the Metropolitan Museum of Art* 30 (February 1935), 39–40.

Dulles, Foster Rhea. *China and America.* Princeton, N.J.: Princeton University Press, 1946.

Duvall, R. Fenton. "Philadelphia's Maritime Commerce with the British Empire." Unpublished Ph.D. dissertation, University of Pennsylvania, 1960.

East, Robert. *Business Enterprise in the American Revolutionary Era.* New York: Columbia University Press, 1938.

Eavenson, Harold. *Two Early Works on Arctic Exploration.* Pittsburgh: no publisher cited, 1946.

Eberlein, Harold and Hubbard, Cortlandt. *Portrait of a Colonial City. Philadelphia: 1670–1838.* Philadelphia: Lippincott, 1939.

Fairbank, John K. "The Legalization of the Opium Trade Before the Treaties of 1858." *Chinese Social and Political Science Review* 17 (July 1933), 215–63.

Fairburn, William. *Merchant Sail.* 6 vols. Center Lovell, Me.: Fairburn Marine Educational Foundation, 1945–55.

Farris, Sara. "Wilmington's Maritime Commerce 1775–1807." *Delaware History* 14, no. 1 (April 1970), 22–51.

Ferguson, Eugene. *Truxton of the Constellation.* Baltimore: Johns Hopkins University Press, 1956.

Fielding, Mantle. *Gilbert Stuart's Portraits of George Washington.* Philadelphia: Printed for the Subscribers, 1923.

Finnie, David. *Pioneers East.* Cambridge: Harvard University Press, 1967.

Fisher, Sidney. *True History of the Revolution.* Philadelphia: Lippincott, 1902.

Forbes, H. A. Crosby. "The American Vision of Cathay," in *Nineteenth Annual Washington Antiques Show/ 1974* (catalogue), pp. 49, 51–54.

Forbes, Henry, Kernan, John, and Wilkins, Ruth. *Chinese Export Silver.* Milton, Mass.: Museum of the American China Trade, 1975.

Forbes, W. Cameron. "Houqua. The Merchant Prince of China 1769–1843." *Bulletin of the American Asiatic Association* 6, no. 6 (1940), 9–18.

Furber, Holden. "The Beginnings of American Trade with India, 1784–1812." *New England Quarterly* 11 (June 1938), 235–65.

Gares, Albert J. "Stephen Girard's West India Trade, 1789–1812." Unpublished D.Ed. dissertation, Teacher's College, Temple University, 1947.

Gates, Edith. "The Washington China." *Quotarian* 10, no. 2 (February 1932), 5–6.

Giesecke, Albert. *American Commercial Policy Before 1789.* New York: Appleton, 1910.

Gillingham, Harold. *Marine Insurance in Philadelphia 1721–1800.* Philadelphia: Privately printed, 1933.

Goldstein, Jonathan. "The China Trade from Philadelphia, 1682–1846: A Study of Interregional Commerce and Cultural Interaction." Ph.D. dissertation, University of Pennsylvania, 1973.

———. "The Ethics of Tribute Versus the Profits of Trade: Stephen Girard's China Trade 1787–1824." Unpublished Senior Honors Thesis, University of Pennsylvania, 1969.

Gorrecht, W. Frank. "Stephen Girard's Connections with Lancaster County." *Historical Papers and Addresses of the Lancaster County Historical Society* 39 (1955), 123–25.

Graham, Edward. "American Ideas of a Special Relationship with China, 1784–1900." Unpublished Ph.D. dissertation, Harvard University, 1968.

Green, Doron. *A History of Bristol Borough.* Bristol, Pa.: Doron Green, 1911.

Greene, Jack. "The 'New History': From Top to Bottom." *New York Times,* January 8, 1975.

Greenberg, Michael. *British Trade and the Opening of China, 1800–1842.* Cambridge: Cambridge University Press, 1951.

Griffis, William. *Corea. The Hermit Nation.* New York: Scribner, 1882.

Hedges, James. *The Browns of Providence Plantation.* 2 vols. Providence, R.I.: Brown University Press, 1968.

Heizer, Robert, and Almquist, Alan. *The Other Californians: Prejudice and Discrimination Under Spain, Mexico, and the United States to 1920.* Berkeley: University of California Press, 1970.

Henderson, Daniel. *Yankee Ships in China Seas.* New York: Hastings House, 1946.

Hendrick, Ulysses. *A History of Agriculture in the State of New York.* Albany: New York State Agricultural Society, 1933.

Hinshaw, William. *Encyclopedia of American Quaker Genealogy.* 2 vols. Ann Arbor, Mich.: Edwards Bros., 1938.

Honour, Hugh. *Chinoiserie: The Vision of Cathay.* London: John Murray, 1961.

Hood, Graham. *Bonnin and Morris of Philadelphia: The First American Porcelain Factory, 1770–1772.* Chapel Hill: University of North Carolina Press, 1972.

Hsu, Immanuel. *China's Entrance into the Family of Nations.* Cambridge: Harvard University Press, 1968.

Hummel, Arthur. "Nathan Dunn." *Quaker History* 59 (Spring 1970), 34–39.

Hummel, Charles. "John Richardson Latimer Comments on the American Scene." *Delaware History* 6 (September 1955), 267–87.

Ingram, Henry. *The Life and Character of Stephen Girard.* Philadelphia: E. Stanley Hart, 1884.

———. *The Life of Jean Girard.* Philadelphia: Edition limited, 1888.

Isaacs, Harold. *Scratches on Our Minds. American Images of China and India.* New York: John Day, 1958.

Jackson, Joseph. *Encyclopedia of Philadelphia.* 4 vols. Harrisburg: National Historical Association, 1933.

Jensen, Arthur. "The Maritime Commerce of Colonial Philadelphia." Ph.D. dissertation, University of Wisconsin, 1954.

Johnson, Emory, Van Metre, T. W., Huebner, G. G., and Hanclett, D. S. *History of Domestic and Foreign Commerce of the United States.* 2 vols. Washington, D.C.: Carnegie Institution of Washington, 1915.

Johnston, Elizabeth. *Original Portraits of Washington.* Boston: James R. Osgood, 1882.

Jones, Brendan. "Ginseng, Seoul's Oldest Export." *New York Times,* March 14, 1971.

Jordan, John, ed. *Colonial Families of Philadelphia.* 2 vols. New York: Lewis Publishing Company, 1911.

Jordan, Winthrop. *White Over Black.* Baltimore: Penguin Books, 1969.

Jourdain, M[argaret]. "The China Trade and Its Influence on Works of Art." *Apollo* 34 (November 1941), 109–11, 114.

———, and Jenyns, R. Soame. *Chinese Export Art in the Eighteenth Century.* London: Spring Books, 1967.

Keyes, Homer. "A Chinese Washington." *Antiques* 15, no. 2 (1929), 109–11.

Kimball, Gertrude. *The East-India Trade of Providence from 1787 to 1807.* Providence: Preston and Rounds, 1896.

King, Frank, and Clarke, Prescott. *A Research Guide to China-Coast Newspapers.* Cambridge: East Asian Research Center, Harvard University, 1965.

Kirschbaum, William. "Famous Old Ship." *The New Bedford Standard,* ca. 1905.

Klopfer, Helen. "Statistics of the Foreign Trade of Philadelphia, 1700–1860." Unpublished Ph.D. dissertation, University of Pennsylvania, 1936.

Labaree, Benjamin. *The Boston Tea Party.* New York: Oxford University Press, 1964.

La Fargue, Thomas. "Some Early Chinese Visitors to the United States." *T'ien Hsia Monthly* 11 (October–November 1949), 128–39.

Lancaster, Clay. "The Chinese Influence in American Architecture and Landscaping." In *Nineteenth Annual Washington Antiques Show/1974* (catalogue), 33–36, 92–94, 97–99.

Latourette, K. S. *The History of Early Relations Between the United States and China.* New Haven: Yale University Press, 1917.

Leach, Frank. "The Philadelphia of Our Ancestors. Old Philadelphia Families." *The North American,* July 7, 1907; March 23, 1913.

Leach, Joseph. *The History of the Girard National Bank of Philadelphia.* Philadelphia: Lippincott, 1902.

Lemisch, Jesse. "Jack Tar in the Streets: Merchant Seamen in the Politics of Revolutionary America." *William and Mary Quarterly,* 3d ser., 14, 3 (July 1968), 373–407.

Liggett, Barbara. *Archaeology at Franklin's Court.* Harrisburg, Pa.: McFarland, 1973.

Lindsay, W. S. *History of Merchant Shipping and Ancient Commerce.* 3 vols. London: Sampson Low, Marston, Low, and Searle, 1876.

Liu, Kwang-Ching. *Anglo-American Steamship Rivalry in China.* Cambridge: Harvard University Press, 1962.

Livingood, James. *The Philadelphia-Baltimore Trade Rivalry, 1780–1860.* Harrisburg: Pennsylvania Historical and Museum Commission, 1947.

Loehr, George. "A. E. Van Braam Houckgeest." *Princeton University Library Chronicle* 15 (Summer 1954), 179–93.

MacDonald, Forrest. *We the People.* Chicago: University of Chicago Press, 1958.

McMaster, John. *The Life and Times of Stephen Girard.* 2 vols. Philadelphia: Lippincott, 1918.

Mason, George. *The Life and Works of Gilbert Stuart.* New York: Scribner, 1879.

Miller, Stuart Creighton. "An East Coast Perspective to Chinese Exclusion, 1852–1882." *The Historian* 33 (February 1971), 183–201.

———. "The Chinese Image in the Eastern United States, 1785–1882." Ph.D. dissertation, Columbia University, 1966.

———. *The Unwelcome Immigrant. The American Image of the Chinese, 1785–1882.* Berkeley: University of California Press, 1969.

Morris, Charles. *Makers of Philadelphia.* Philadelphia: L. R. Hamersly, 1894.

Morse, Hosea. *The Chronicles of the East India Company.* 5 vols. Oxford: Oxford University Press, 1926.

———. *The Gilds of China.* London: Longmans, Green, 1909.

———. *The International Relations of the Chinese Empire.* 2 vols. London: Longmans, Green, 1910.

———. "The Provision of Funds for the East India Company's Trade." *Journal of the Royal Asiatic Society,* Part II (April 1922), 227–55.

———, and Macnair, Harley. *Far Eastern International Relations.* Boston: Houghton Mifflin, 1931.

Morton, Thomas, and Woodbury, Frank. *History of the Pennsylvania Hospital.* Philadelphia: Times Printing House, 1895.

Mudge, Jean. *Chinese Export Porcelain for the American Trade. 1785–1835.* Newark: University of Delaware Press, 1972.

Myers, Gustavus. *History of the Great American Fortunes.* New York: Modern Library, 1937.

Oberholtzer, Ellis. *Philadelphia: A History of the City and Its People.* 4 vols. Philadelphia: S. J. Clarke Publishing Company, 1912.

Owen, David. *British Opium Policy in China and India.* New Haven: Yale University Press, 1934.

Packard, Francis. *Some Account of the Pennsylvania Hospital.* Philadelphia: Engle Press, 1938.

Paullin, Charles. *Diplomatic Negotiations of American Naval Officers.* Baltimore: Johns Hopkins Press, 1912.

Phillips, Clifton. *Protestant America and the Pagan World.* Cambridge: Harvard University Press, 1969.

Pickowicz, Paul. "William Wood in Canton." *EIHC* 107 (January 1971), 3–34.

Porter, Kenneth. *John Jacob Astor. Business Man.* 2 vols. Cambridge: Harvard University Press, 1931.

Ranshaw, Carol. "Calendar of the University of Delaware Collection of the John Latimer China Trade Papers." Unpublished Master's thesis, School of Library Science, Drexel Institute of Technology, 1953.

Richardson, E. P. "China Trade Portraits of Washington After Stuart." *PMHB* 94 (January 1970), 95–100.

Rivinus, Marion, and Biddle, Katharine Hansell. *Lights Along the Delaware.* Philadelphia: Dorrance & Co., 1965.

Rochemonteix, Camille de. *Les Jésuites et la Nouvelle-France au XVIIᵉ Siècle,* vol. III. Paris: Letouzey et Ané, 1896.

Roth, Rodris. *Floor Coverings in 18th-Century America.* Washington, D.C.: Smithsonian Institution Press, 1967.

———. *Tea Drinking in 18th-Century America.* Washington, D.C.: Smithsonian Institution, 1961.

Saxton, Alexander. *The Indispensable Enemy: Labor and the Anti-Chinese Movement in California.* Berkeley: University of California Press, 1971.

Scharf, James. *History of Delaware 1609–1888.* 2 vols. Philadelphia: L. J. Richards, 1888.

Scharf, J. Thomas, and Wescott, Thompson. *History of Philadelphia 1609–1884.* 3 vols. Philadelphia: L. H. Everts, 1884.

Seebohm, Benjamin. *Memoirs of the Life and Gospel Labors of Stephen Grellet.* 2 vols. London: A. W. Bennett, 1860.

Seltzer, Ruth. "The Best of Two Old River Houses Is Combined in Knauer Residence." *Evening Bulletin* (Philadelphia), December 10, 1957, p. 58.

Shinn, Henry. *The History of Mount Holly.* Mount Holly, N.J.: Privately printed, 1957.

Small, Samuel. *Genealogical Records of George Small.* Philadelphia: Lippincott, 1905.

Smith, F. Porter. *Chinese Materia Medica.* Revised by G. A. Stuart. Shanghai: American Presbyterian Mission Press, 1911.

Solis-Cohen, Berta. "Philadelphia's Expeditions to Labrador." *PH* 19 (April 1952), 148–62.

Souder, Casper. *The History of Chestnut Street.* Philadelphia: *Sunday Dispatch,* 1858.

Sparks, Jared. *Life of John Ledyard, the American Traveller.* Boston: Charles C. Little and James Brown, 1847.

Speer, William. *The Oldest and the Newest Empire.* Hartford: S. S. Scranton, 1870.

Spoehr, Luther. "Sambo and the Heathen Chinee: Californians' Racial Stereotypes in the Late 1870's." *PHR* 42 (May 1973), 185–204.

Stanton, William. *The Leopard's Spots: Scientific Attitudes Toward Race in America.* Chicago: University of Chicago Press, 1960.

Stelle, Charles. "American Opium Trade to China Prior to 1820." *PHR* 9 (December 1940), 425–44.

Sweeney, John. *The Treasure House of Early American Rooms.* New York: Viking Press, 1963.

Symons, Van Jay. "The Ch'ing Ginseng Monopoly." Unpublished Ph.D. dissertation, Brown University, 1975.

Taussig, Frank. *The Tariff History of the United States.* 5th ed. New York: Putnam, 1910 [1892].

Taylor, Thomas. "Philadelphia's Counterpart of the Boston Tea Party." *Bulletin of the Friends Historical Society of Philadelphia* 2 (November 1908), 86–100.

Thill, Joan. "A Delawarean in the Celestial Empire." Unpublished M.A. Thesis, University of Delaware, 1973.

Thorpe, Janet. "Chinoiserie in America with Emphasis on the Van Braam Houckgeest Collection." Term Paper, Institute of Fine Arts, New York University, May 1964.

Tong, Te-kong. *United States Diplomacy in China, 1844–60.* Seattle: University of Washington Press, 1964.

Tsiang, T. F. "The Extension of Equal Commercial Privileges to Other Nations After the Treaty of Nanking." *Chinese Social and Political Science Review* 15 (October 1931), 422–44.

University Hospital Antiques Show/1972 (catalog).

Van Alstyne, Richard. *The Rising American Empire.* New York: Oxford University Press, 1960.

Ver Steeg, Clarence. "Financing and Outfitting the First United States Ship to China." *PHR* 22 (February 1953), 1–12.

Waln, Nora. *The House of Exile.* Boston: Little, Brown, 1933.

Walzer, John. "Colonial Philadelphia and Its Backcountry." *Winterthur Portfolio* 7 (1972), 161–73.

Wetmore, James. *The Wetmore Family of America.* Albany: Munsell & Rowland, 1861.

White, Ann. "The China Trade from Philadelphia, 1785–1820." Unpublished M.A. research paper, University of Pennsylvania, 1962.

———. "The Hong Merchants of Canton." Unpublished Ph.D. dissertation, University of Pennsylvania, 1968.

Wildes, Harry. *Lonely Midas.* New York: Farrar & Rinehart, 1943.

[Winslow, Stephen J.] *Biographies of Successful Philadelphia Merchants.* Philadelphia: James K. Simon, 1864.

Winsor, Justin. *Narrative and Critical History of America.* Boston: Houghton Mifflin, 1886.

Wright, Walter. "American Relations with Turkey to 1831." Unpublished Ph.D. dissertation, Princeton University, 1928.

Chinese cotton tree

Index